Schwerpunktthema

Abitur Englisch

An Inconvenient Truth

A Film Study

Cornelsen

An Inconvenient Truth: A Film Study

von Christiane Mayer

Verlagsredaktion

Neil Porter

Layout und technische Umsetzung

May + Steinmüller, Designbureau, Berlin

Umschlaggestaltung

hawemannundmosch, Konzeption und Gestaltung, Berlin

www.cornelsen.de

1. Auflage, 1. Druck 2011

Alle Drucke dieser Auflage sind inhaltlich unverändert und können im Unterricht nebeneinander verwendet werden.

Druck: Firmengruppe APPL, aprinta druck, Wemding

ISBN 978-3-06-032574-0

Inhalt gedruckt auf säurefreiem Papier aus nachhaltiger Forstwirtschaft.

Contents

Liebe Schülerinnen und Schüler,

in diesem Heft finden Sie Vorschläge zur Auseinandersetzung mit dem Dokumentarfilm *An Inconvenient Truth* von Davis Guggenheim mit dem ehemaligen Vizepräsidenten und Präsidentschaftskandidaten Al Gore über globale Erwärmung.

Eine Beschäftigung mit dem Film lohnt schon wegen der Aktualität des Themas, und weil er neben den beiden Oskars für den besten Dokumentarfilm und den besten Song als erster Film seit 10 Jahren auch einen Special-Humanitas Preis für seine besonders gelungene Botschaft an die Menschheit erhielt.

Bei dieser Botschaft handelt es sich um Gores Appell an die Zuschauer und vor allem auch an aktive Politiker, sich für den Klimaschutz einzusetzen und dringend notwenige Maßnahmen zu ergreifen. Hierzu stellt er seine Sicht auf den derzeitigen Stand der Klimaforschung dar und verdeutlicht die Folgen, die die globale Erwärmung schon jetzt hat und – wenn wir eine Fortsetzung des Prozesses nicht schnellstens beenden – auch weiterhin haben wird. Eine „unbequeme Wahrheit" eben. Unter anderem nennt er:

- das Abschmelzen der Gletscher, zum Teil mit dramatischen Folgen für die Trinkwasserversorgung
- Überschwemmungen durch sturzflutartige Regenmengen in kleineren Gebieten und gleichzeitiges Austrocknen benachbarter Gebiete
- das Auftauen des Permafrostbodens in der Arktis
- das Abschmelzen der Eiskappen an den Polen und dadurch drohende Überschwemmung von küstennahen Gebieten mit verheerenden Folgen für die dort lebenden Menschen
- die Zunahme von Hurrikans und Tornados
- die Konsequenzen des Klimawandels für die Fauna

Interessant ist die Beschäftigung mit dem Film aber auch aufgrund seiner Rezeption. Zwar bestätigen viele Klimatologen die Richtigkeit von Gores Argumentation, andere kritisieren den Film aber wegen mangelnder Wissenschaftlichkeit. Unter anderem wird Gore vorgeworfen, zu wenig auf die notwendigen und möglichen Maßnahmen zum Klimaschutz einzugehen und stattdessen *worst-case*-Szenarien ohne zeitliche Einordnung zu verwenden. So würde das komplette Abschmelzen der Eiskappen und der damit verbundene Anstieg des Meeresspiegels um mehrere Meter nach heutigem Kenntnisstand mindestens einige tausend Jahre dauern und nicht – wie im Film suggeriert – in „naher Zukunft" eintreten. Dies ist einer von 9 angeblichen Fehlern, die zur Entscheidung eines britischen Gerichtes führten, dass der Film in Schulen nur gezeigt werden darf, wenn die Schüler auf diese Fehler aufmerksam gemacht werden. Ein Hauptkritikpunkt von Gegnern des Films ist aber vor allem, dass Al Gore seinen eigenen Lebensstil in keiner Weise an seine Forderungen anpasst. Aus diesen Standpunkten können sich nach der Auseinandersetzung mit diesen sicherlich interessante Diskussionen im Unterricht ergeben.

Zur Arbeit mit dem Film enthält das Themenheft nach *Pre-Watching Tasks and Activities*, in denen Sie Ihre Vorkenntnisse zum Thema aktivieren sollen, zunächst einen *Scene Index*, der das Auffinden von Szenen erleichtert.

Die *While-Watching Tasks and Activities* enthalten Aufgaben zu den einzelnen Filmszenen. Hier stehen das Verständnis des Films, Al Gores Argumentation und die filmischen Mittel im Vordergrund. Die Fragen beziehen sich aber auch zum Teil schon auf die kritische Auseinandersetzung mit dem Film und Gores Argumentation. Selbstverständlich müssen die Aufgaben nicht alle bearbeitet werden, sondern Sie können für sich selbst Schwerpunkte setzen.

Im Kapitel *Background Information* finden Sie Hintergrundinformationen zu Ereignissen, die von Gore im Film angesprochen werden und die für dessen Verständnis von Bedeutung sein könnten.

Im Anschluss daran geht es im Kapitel *After Watching the Film* um eine kritische Auseinandersetzung mit dem Film und dessen Argumentation. In diesem Zusammenhang wird auch dessen Rezeption thematisiert. Es bietet sich an, eine UNO-Resolution zum Thema zu schreiben oder eine Diskussion mit „Al Gore auf dem heißen Stuhl" zu simulieren.

Abgeschlossen wird die inhaltliche Arbeit mit dem Film im Kapitel *Beyond the Film* durch aktuelle Texte zum Thema.

Das Filmheft ist so angelegt, dass Sie sich den Film eigenständig erarbeiten können. Falls Ihnen eine Aufgabe Schwierigkeiten bereitet, schauen Sie nach unter www.cornelsen.de/abi-e (dort das Cover des Heftes anclicken). Die Anmerkungen, die Sie dort abrufen und für sich überprüfen können, sind nicht einfach als „richtige" Lösungen gedacht, sondern als Wegweiser für Ihre Arbeit.

Unter derselben Adresse finden Sie zur Diskussion der filmischen Präsentation der Themen auch das *Worksheet Selected terms for film analysis* zum Nachschlagen der wichtigsten Film-Termini.

Gutes Gelingen wünscht Ihnen

Christiane Mayer

Pre-Watching Tasks and Activities

■ 1

a) Describe the cartoon, and explain its message.
b) Speculate why the title of the film is *An Inconvenient Truth*.
c) Explain who the truth might be inconvenient for.

■ 2 The film *An Inconvenient Truth* is a documentary film directed by Davis Guggenheim about Al Gore's campaign to educate citizens about global warming.

a) Jot down what you know about Al Gore and try to find out more about him.
b) Explain what the cartoon tells you about him.

■ **3** What do you know about global warming? Jot down your ideas and try to classify them.

Reasons for global warming	**Consequences of global Warming**	**Possible Solutions for the problem**

Scene Index

Chapter (Time)	Contents
1	**The River 0:00:36–0:06:20**
0:00:34–0:01:20	An idyllic and peaceful picture of a river can be seen; a voice from off-camera comments on it and later complains that we tend to forget about this beautiful aspect of nature.
0:01:21–0:02:41	Preparation of Gore's lecture on global warming and the environmental movement; cross-cut to the listeners of a lecture about the Apollo 8 mission and his (lost) presidential campaign in 2000.
0:02:42–0:04:13	Gore travelling in his car with a notebook; he explains that he has been trying to protect the environment for a long time; cross-cuts between Gore in his car and pictures of natural catastrophes such as droughts, melting ice caps, power stations polluting the air and hurricanes (especially hurricane "Katrina").
0:04:14–0:06:20	Gore continues his lecture about the beginning of the environmental movement; he explains that it all started with the first pictures of the earth from space, which were taken during and after the Apollo 8 mission on Christmas Eve 1968.
2	**Continental Drift 0:06:21–0:08:31**
0:06:21–0:07:35	Gore tells a story about his geography teacher – who ridiculed a student that asked if the east coast of South America and the west coast of Africa ever fitted together; however, he explains that the teacher was just reflecting the conclusion of the scientific establishment of that time and emphasizes that we now know better. From this he draws the conclusion that *"what gets us into trouble is not what we don't know. It's what we know for sure that just ain't so"* (Mark Twain).
0:07:36–0:08:31	He compares this wrong assumption of the past with an – equally wrong – assumption about global warming: "The earth is so big, we can't possibly have any lasting harmful impact on the earth's environment" and points out that this assumption is wrong because of the thinness of the global atmosphere.
3	**Basic Science of Global Warming 0:08:32–0:09:29**
0:08:32–0:09:29	Gore explains the basics of global warming with the help of a diagram.
4	**Global Warming Cartoon 0:09:30–0:11:20**
0:09:30–0:11:10	In a cartoon an adult explains global warming to a little girl whose ice-cream has melted due to the heat; it is suggested that one futile way to fight global warming in 2068 could be to throw large ice cubes into the oceans to reduce the temperature; this would supposedly "solve the problem once and for all".
5	**Professor Revelle 0:11:21–0:13:30**
0:11:21–0:13:30	Gore gives a character portrait of Professor Revelle and explains his methods of measuring the concentration of carbon dioxide in the atmosphere; moreover, he underlines his personal fondness and respect for his professor and his work.
6	**CO_2 Measure Since 1958 0:13:31–0:15:44**
0:13:31–0:14:22	He gives background information on the graph: He explains that although the graph is actually moving upwards continually, it is going up and down once a year because the vast majority of the land masses and most of the vegetation is north of the equator; so when the northern hemisphere is tilted towards the sun the leaves breath in CO_2 and the amount of it in the atmosphere goes down, whereas when the northern hemisphere is tilted away from the sun the leaves fall and exhale CO_2.
0:14:23–0:15:42	Gore mentions his efforts to bring global warming onto the political agenda. In the background the graph can be seen moving up over the years.

Chapter (Time)	Contents
7	**Glaciers Recede 0:15:45–0:17:49**
0:15:43–0:16:31	Gore starts explaining the impact of global warming on the world. He shows past and present pictures of Kilimanjaro and explains what a friend of his, who studies glaciers, has found out. He shows more past and present pictures of other glaciers in America (Glacier National Park, Columbia Glacier).
0:16:32–0:17:13	He draws the conclusion that the fact that the glaciers are melting away is a shame because they are beautiful, but emphasizes that this is also a serious problem because it will lead to a serious shortage of drinking water for 40% of the people in the world.
0:17:14–0:17:49	He shows past and present pictures of other glaciers (in the Alps, South America).
8	**Ice Cores 0:17:50–0:19:32**
0:17:50–0:18:30	Gore explains how scientists measure the temperature and the amount of CO_2 in the air with the help of core drilling into the ice.
0:18:31–0:18:47	He informs the audience that core drills in the Antarctic reveal that the Clean Air Act of 1970 has led to major improvements.
0:18:48–0:19:33	He shows the thermometer of the temperature that was reconstructed for the last 1,000 years with the help of core drills into the ice and proves the people wrong who deny the impact of global warming by claiming that this is a cyclical phenomenon and that there was a medieval warming period, too.
9	**CO_2 Levels Back 650,000 Years 0:19:34–0:23:51**
0:19:34–0:21:41	He shows the relationship between temperature and CO_2 concentrations in the last 1,000 years. To prove his thesis he shows the same relationship on graphs that illustrate the temperature and the CO_2 concentration during the last 650,000 years. Moreover, he underlines that the CO_2 concentration has never gone above 300 parts per million within the last 650,000 years.
0:21:42–0:23:51	He explains that the concentration of CO_2 is already much higher than it has ever been over the last 650,000 years and predicts where it will be within less than 50 years. Then he underlines our responsibility for the problem. Furthermore, he claims that this is not so much a political but a moral problem.
10	**Albert's Accident 0:23:52–0:26:59**
0:23:52–0:24:46	Gore expresses his disappointment with the political system and other politicians.
0:24:47–0:26:59	He tells the story about his son's serious accident and his slow but successful recovery. He explains that because of his son's accident he wanted to help improve the world in order to make sure that everything that we take for granted will still be there for our children (picture of the river from the beginning can be seen again).
11	**Rising Temperatures 0:27:00–0:28:51**
0:27:00–0:28:18	On the basis of a graph Gore explains again that the rise of temperature has been uninterrupted and intensifying in recent years; to underline the impact of this he shows pictures of heat waves throughout the world (Europe, India and America) and mentions the number of deaths that were caused by them.
0:28:19–0:28:51	He explains that with the rise of the world temperature the temperature of the oceans also increases.
12	**Hurricanes 0:28:52–0:32:51**
0:28:52–0:29:55	On the basis of concrete examples he argues that the number and force of hurricanes, tornadoes and typhoons has increased within the last years and that they even have occurred in places where they were thought impossible. Moreover, he shows the damage they did to the oil industry.

Chapter (Time)	Contents
0:29:56–0:30:41	He describes how hurricane Katrina, which hit Florida "only" as a Category One hurricane, could gain force when moving over warm water and then caused the national catastrophe in New Orleans.
0:30:42–0:31:36	He shows pictures of the situation in New Orleans shortly after the hurricane had hit the city.
0:31:37–0:32:13	He asks how this could happen in America and complains that people do not listen to the warnings of the scientists.
0:32:14–0:32:51	He refers back to a storm in Europe in 1930 that Winston Churchill warned about. When people refused to listen to him he said that "the era of procrastination, of half-measures, of soothing and baffling expedients, of delays is coming to its close. In its place we are entering a period of consequences."
13	**2000 Election 0:32:52–0:35:20**
0:32:52–0:33:12	Gore can be seen on a plane looking down at the earth; from off-camera he explains that whereas past mistakes could have been made up for, this – unfortunately – is no longer possible now.
0:33:13–0:33:19	A newsreader says that despite Gore being the winner of the national vote, whoever wins Florida will be president.
0:33:20–0:34:01	Pictures of the counting of votes in Florida, of press conferences, court hearings, etc. can be seen.
0:34:02–0:34:36	Gore announces that he accepts the outcome of the election. And we see pictures of George W. Bush and the first days of his presidency.
0:34:37–0:35:20	Gore admits, though, that his defeat was hard to accept. However, he decided to give lectures about global warming again.
14	**Precipitation and Evaporation 0:35:21–0:37:51**
0:35:21–0:36:24	He explains that global warming also leads to an increase of precipitation, but that most of this comes in one-off big storms and that these in the long run cause more damage. To prove his claim the viewers can see pictures of floods around the world (Switzerland, Mumbai, China).
0:36:25–0:37:27	He argues that global warming also causes evaporation because it relocates precipitation. As proof the viewers see pictures of Darfur, Niger and Lake Chad in the Sahara.
0:37:28–0:37:51	He explains that the reason for this is that global warming increases evaporation of the oceans and also dramatically increases moisture evaporation out of the soil.
15	**The Gore Farm 0:37:52–0:40:03**
0:37:52–0:39:34	Gore drives back to his parent's farm and remembers that as a child he was in close contact with nature; old photographs and pictures of nature can be seen.
0:39:35–0:40:03	He explains that the climate pattern on his parent's farm is changing relatively quickly now, although it did not change much in the last 11,000 years.
16	**The Arctic 0:40:04–0:44:06**
0:40:04–0:41:42	He explains the major consequences global warming has on the Arctic.
0:41:43–0:42:38	He explains that the thickness of the ice at the North Pole has been measured with a nuclear submarine since 1957 and that its thickness has diminished by 40% in 40 years. He predicts that within the next 50–70 years there will be no more ice left in summer.
0:42:39–0:43:29	He argues that with the melting of the ice there is less ice that can "work like a mirror" and reflect the sun; instead the bigger amount of water absorbs a larger amount of sunrays and the heat increases.

Chapter (Time)	Contents
0:43:30–0:44:06	He states that this has a major impact on polar bears, many of which have drowned because they could not find ice; he asks what impact the increasing amount of water has on us.
17	**The Ocean Conveyer 0:44:07–0:47:24**
0:44:07–0:45:03	He answers his own question by explaining that the Earth's climate is like a big engine for redistributing heat by means of water and wind currents; because of this an average increase of worldwide temperature by 5° would lead to an increase of just 1° at the equator and 12° at the poles; and this would lead to a change of the – so far relatively stable – currents.
0:45:04–0:47:24	With the help of an animation he explains how the water currents work in the North Atlantic, where the Gulf Stream evaporates so that its heat is carried over Europe; as a consequence the remaining colder and saltier water sinks and is pulled back south. Then he reminds the viewer of the fact that at the end of the last Ice Age the melting of an ice-cap in North America stopped this process, leading to another ice age for Europe. While Gore is ironically claiming that this – of course – will never happen again, the camera shows the map of Greenland which is covered with ice.
18	**Resistance to Change 0:47:25–0:49:22**
0:47:25–0:48:21	At the airport Gore complains that despite his efforts the USA is still the worst contributor to the problem and that there are no signs for a change.
0:48:22–0:48:58	While Gore can be seen entering his plane, politicians (among them George W. Bush) can be seen; all of them question the seriousness of the problem and mention the negative impact an environment-friendly policy would have on the American economy.
0:48:59–0:49:22	Gore complains (to himself) that the problem is not taken seriously by the politicians
19	**Troubling Signs 0:49:23–0:52:04**
0:48:54–0:50:12	Gore shows the impact of global warming.
20	**Antarctica 0:52:05–0:54:58**
0:52:05–0:52:40	He quotes a friend of his who said in 1978 that if one sees the break-up of ice shelves along the Antarctic peninsula, then that should be seen as an alarm bell for global warming and then shows how much ice has broken up in recent years.
0:52:41–0:54:19	With the example of Larson Ice Shelf Gore illustrates how a great amount of ice completely disappeared within just 35 days; he explains that the pools of melting water that form within the ice are responsible for this; moreover, when the floating ice cracks, it can no longer hold back the land-based ice
0:54:20–0:54:58	He makes it clear that the melting of land-based ice causes sea-level rise and underlines the seriousness of the problem by showing pictures of people who had to be evacuated during a flood.
21	**Sea-level Rise 0:54:59–0:58:46**
0:54:59–0:55:23	He explains that if either the West Antarctic Ice Shelf or Greenland melted, they would raise sea levels by 20 feet.
0:55:24–0:56:45	He shows pictures of pools of melting water in Greenland and explains that these pools "dig" tunnels into the ice and destroy it; although he admits that this has always been happening he underlines that the process has been intensifying in recent years.

Chapter (Time)	Contents
0:56:46–0:57:59	He points out the consequences the melting of Greenland would have on Florida, San Francisco Bay, the Netherlands, Beijing, Shanghai, Calcutta, Bangladesh.
0:58:00–0:58:46	He shows the impact the melting of Greenland would have on Manhattan and warns viewers that terrorism is not the only threat to modern life.
22	**China 0:58:47–1:00:56**
0:58:47–1:00:56	Gore can be seen together with scientists in China; he points out that both the USA and China rely on old, polluting technologies and that the consequences of this will affect both countries alike; therefore solutions must be sought together.
23	**Population Explosion 1:00:57–1:02:37**
1:00:57–1:02:04	He explains that the exploding population of the Earth (from 2 billion to 9 billion in his lifetime) puts pressure on it because of increasing food and water demand and an increasing demand on natural resources.
1:02:05–1:02:37	He adds that cutting down trees is not the only problem: forest and brush fires – especially in developing countries – produce about 30 % of the CO_2 that goes up into the atmosphere every year.
24	**Old Habits + New Technology 1:02:38–1:06:43**
1:02:38–1:03:44	Although he admits that we profit from new technologies, he warns people not to merely continue old habits with new technologies: to illustrate his thesis he shows the development of warfare with spears and arrows to the nuclear bomb.
1:03:45–1:05:03	He argues that the same applies to the exploitation of the earth; whereas tools have long been very simple and had no lasting effect on the surface of the earth, the diversion of rivers for irrigation with modern tools in more recent times has led to the drying out of the Aral Sea or the Colorado River.
1:05:04–1:05:42	He shows the contributions of the different countries to global warming; the USA is responsible for 30,3 %, the same as Asia, South America, the Middle East and Africa combined; this is still true when the contribution per capita is considered.
1:05:43- 1:06:43	He appeals to the audience to become aware of the danger of and to start doing something against global warming.
25	**Working Tobacco 1:06:44–1:09:12**
1:06:44–1:09:12	He tells us that his family kept growing tobacco despite the connection between lung cancer and smoking tobacco that became known in 1964; they decided to stop, however, after Gore's older sister died of lung cancer, because they understood that they had been part of the industry that produced the cancer. He expresses his regret that they didn't understand this earlier.
26	**Is There A Controversy? 1:09:13–1:10:51**
1:09:13–1:10:51	He emphasizes that there is no disagreement among scientists that the problem of global warming is real and that we are causing it, but that about 50 % of the articles in the popular press doubt it and that is why people are confused.
27	**Science Fraud 1:10:52–1:13:53**
1:10:52–1:12:52	He suggests that, just like in the former Soviet Union, scientists might be put under pressure by George W. Bush's government to deny unpleasant facts and commit science fraud.
1:12:53–1:13:40	He talks about Philip Cooney who used to work for the petroleum industry and was then hired as Chief of Staff for the Environmental Office of the White House; despite having no scientific training, he changed a memo on global warming; when this became public knowledge he resigned and started working for Exxon Mobile.

Chapter (Time)	Contents
1:13:41–1:13:53	He recalls a statement by Upton Sinclair, who said about 100 years ago: "It is difficult to get a man to understand something when his salary depends upon him not understanding it."
28	**Balancing the Ecomomy and Environment 1:13:54–1:15:23**
1:13:54–1:15:23	He argues that we do not have to make a choice between the economy and the environment, because if we make the right choices we can create jobs and the economy can profit from that.
29	**City by City 1:15:24–1:18:52**
1:15:24–1:17:24	He explains that the only way to change people's minds is to travel from city to city and give his slide show.
1:17:25–1:18:52	He claims that higher mileage standards on cars do not threaten the economy, but with them more cars could be sold because they would meet international standards; American companies are in trouble because they do not meet the standards.
30	**The Solutions are in Our Hands 1:18:53–1:21:54**
1:18:53 - 1:20:01	While many people despair about global warming, Gore points out that "humanity already possesses the fundamental scientific, technical, and industrial know-how to solve the carbon and climate problems ..." (Stephen Pacala and Robert Socolow, 2004) and explains that the solution is to reduce CO_2 to a level below the 1970 emissions.
1:20:02–1:20:15	He admits that maybe political will is lacking; but at the same time he reminds the audience that political will in America is a renewable resource.
1:20:16–1:20:35	He reminds each listener of their personal responsibility and explains what people can do.
1:20:36–1:21:25	He informs the viewers about the fact that all advanced nations except for the USA and Australia have ratified Kyoto. However, he points out that several American states and cities are taking the initiative.
31	**Are We Capable of Doing Great Things? 1:21:26–1:23:11**
1:21:26–1:23:11	He expresses his conviction that the nations of the world are capable of solving the problem; to convince his listeners he mentions achievements from the past.
32	**Our Only Home 1:23:12–1:25:58**
1:23:12–1:24:30	Once again, he emphasizes that it is our moral responsibility to save our planet.
1:24:31–1:25:59	Idyllic pictures of nature can be seen; Gore suggests that future generations might reproach us for not waking up when we had a chance.
33	**Final Appeal and Credits 1:25:59**
1:25:59–1:32:36	An internet address can be seen: www.climatecrisis.net

Topics to Concentrate on

These activities should be done while watching the video. Basically they serve to help you analyze the content, the argumentative structure of the film and filmic devices.

■ **Content:**
In order to remember and to structure the information provided in the film you should copy and fill in the following grid while watching the film for the first time.

The impact of climate change on	Recent changes (outline main ideas and try to add some facts and figures that support them)	Names of places that are worst affected
Glaciers		
World air temperature		
Hurricanes and storms		
Rainfall, evaporation and drought		
The Arctic region		
Antarctica		
Biodiversity and where and how things live		
Sea-level rise and inhabited areas		

■ **Analysis and discussion:**
You will find the 5 major topics and the corresponding chapters in the boxes on the following pages. After watching the scenes in detail, it might be worth discussing some of the questions. You should, of course, concentrate on certain chapters and not answer all the questions here. Depending on the topic you want to concentrate on, you can focus on the corresponding chapters for close analysis (cf. tasks for the different chapters, pp. 18–28).

Topic 1

Basic information about climate change (Chapters 3, 4, 5 and 6)

Questions to be discussed after watching (a selection of) these scenes:

- Why do you think climate change matters?
- Have the scenes helped you to understand the issue?
- How does the issue relate to your personal life?
- What part do you feel you have played in the rise of CO_2 levels? What do you think you personally could do differently?
- What solutions does the film suggest for the problem? Do you think they are enough to stop global warming?

  You can also use the following sites to measure student and school contributions to carbon: www.carbondetectives.org.uk or www.esd.rgs.org.

Topic 2

The role of the media and the science community – have they helped or hindered public understanding? (Chapters 18, 25, 26, 27)

Questions to be discussed after watching (a selection of) these scenes:

- What lessons can be learned from the way that tobacco has been presented in the media?
- Does the media have a responsibility to only present facts about climate change – or should it also comment on the arguments? What are the implications for the role of the media?
- Whose role is it to make new scientific findings accessible to the general public? That of the scientists or of the government?
- What are the implications of the statement: "Reposition global warming as theory rather than fact."
- Explore the way in which *An Inconvenient Truth* deals with facts and argument. Should the film have included more evidence to support Gore's conclusions?
- How does the use of emotive material, and departures from mainstream scientific opinion, help Gore get his message across? Is this appropriate in this film?
- Is *An Inconvenient Truth* – in your opinion – a scientific film?

Topic 3

The role of the politicians (Chapters 13, 18, 23, 24, 27)

Questions to be discussed after watching (a selection of) these scenes:

- The film suggests that it would have been better if Gore (instead of Bush) had been elected president. Analyze how this is made clear with the help of filmic devices.
- Consider the reasons why politicians may have chosen not to act on climate change.
- Gore claims in the film that combating climate change is an issue as important as fighting terrorism. Do you agree?
- What decisions might politicians have to make in response to climate change?
- Should politicians take the lead on climate change? Is it an issue that can be legislated about?
- Are politicians responsible to their own electorate or the international community? What are the consequences of these responsibilities?
- Should we be taking action on climate change? How can people who want to take action (or people who oppose such action) use the democratic system to achieve their aims?

Useful websites:
www.bbc.co.uk/climate/policies/kyoto.shtml; www.whitehouse.gov/energy/climate-change

Topic 4

Al Gore's lifetime and personal narrative (Chapters 2, 3, 5, 11, 15, 29)

Questions to be discussed after watching (a selection of) these scenes:

- Gore can always be seen with his notebook. Explain why the director of the film might have made this decision.
- Gore frequently mentions friends of his who photographed or studied environmental phenomena. Explain the effect this has on the viewer.
- Apart from global warming we also learn much about Gore's personal life. Explain what we learn and why these scenes have been included in the film.
- Why does Al Gore use his own life as a narrative to hold this documentary together?
- Are there any benefits to having the science explained over one person's lifetime or is it a distraction from the hard science?
- Does having a politician rather than a scientist or journalist present this material help us understand it better? Does it detract from the objectivity of the film?
- Do Gore's efforts to get people to learn about climate change tell us anything about the issues?
- Would it be possible to map the changes to the climate to our own lives – starting with what we know about it and when we found out?

Topic 5

The industrialization of the developing world (Chapters 22, 23, 24)

Questions to be discussed after watching (a selection of) these scenes:

- The industrialization of the developed world (Europe, USA) led to the rise in carbon emissions. Do we have a right to stop developing countries from doing the same thing? Or do they have a right to advance technologically just as the developed world did – even now that we know about the consequences for the environment.
- In what way can the developing world be assisted by the developed world?
- Whose responsibility is it to galvanize the international community to cooperate and share technologies?

While-Watching Tasks and Activities

1 THE RIVER 0:00:36–0:06:20

1. Explain the function of the introductory passage of the film (the pictures of the river on Gore's farm; [0:00:34–0:01:20]) within its argumentative structure.

2. Analyze the filmic devices that are used to create this idyllic picture of nature.

3. Analyze the filmic devices that are used to point out that Gore is a very popular person and that people are interested in his message [0:01:23–0:02:41].

0:04:28

4. Explain the function of the pictures of the 2000 election and of Gore's comment 'I am Al Gore – I used to be the next president of the Unites States of America. [Laughter of the audience]. I don't find that particularly funny.' [0:02:16]

5. Describe the different effects of global warming and pollution that can be seen in the pictures [0:02:42–0:04:13]. Analyze how the growing threat of global warming and Gore's concern about this is underlined with the help of filmic devices.

6. Gore claims that with the first picture of the earth, which was taken on the Apollo 8 mission on Christmas Eve 1968, the environmental movement had begun. Explain why this picture had such a great impact.

2 CONTINENTAL DRIFT 0:06:21–0:08:31

1. Summarize what happened during the geography lesson Gore recalls.

2. Explain the function of this story within the film. In doing so also explain Gore's quotation from Mark Twain that "what gets us into trouble is not what we don't know. It´s what we know for sure that just ain't so."

3. Discuss wether you agree with this quotation or not. If you do, relate it to other situations to which it applies.

3	BASIC SCIENCE OF GLOBAL WARMING 0:08:32–0:09:29

1. Explain the basic facts about global warming on the basis of this still.
2. Describe the still. What impression of Gore is achieved here? How?

0:09:29

4	GLOBAL WARMING CARTOON 0:09:30–0:11:20

1. Explain the function of this cartoon within the argumentative structure of the film.

5	PROFESSOR REVELLE 0:11:21–0:13:30

1. Summarize Professor Revelle's scientific achievements.
2. Gore claims that Professor Revelle and his colleagues worked very precisely for decades. Analyze how this claim is underlined with the help of filmic devices.
3. Analyze what impression of Gore is created in this passage with the help of filmic devices.

6	CO_2 MEASURE SINCE 1958 0:13:31–0:15:44

1. Explain why the amount of carbon dioxide in the air goes up and down every year.
2. Analyze how, with the help of filmic devices, the danger of the increasing amount of carbon dioxide is made clear to the viewer.
3. Gore explicitly says that he started to do something about the problem very early on. Summarize what he did.

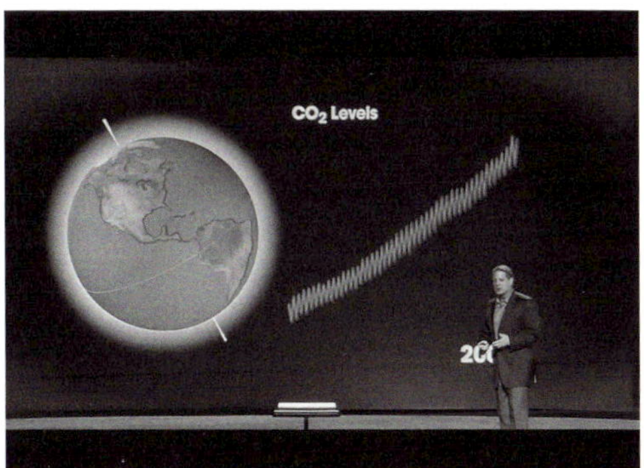

0:15:40

7 GLACIERS RECEDE 0:15:45–0:17:49

1. Analyze how the impact that global warming has on glaciers is underlined with the help of filmic devices.

2. Explain what other problem occurs with the melting of the glaciers.

8 ICE CORES 0:17:50–0:19:32

1. **Close viewing:** Listen to what Gore says about core drilling into the ice and complete the sentences.

A Al Gore explains that when snow falls, it …
B That is why they can measure how much … in the year that this snow fell.
C Moreover, they can figure out a very precise … by …
D When one looks at the core drills, one can see with the naked eye, when the US Congress …
E One can count back year by year, just as the …
F You can see each … from the …
G Sceptics of global warming claim that the rise of temperature is a …, because there also was a …
H When one looks back at 1000 years of temperature and 1000 years of CO_2 concentration, one can see …

2. Explain to what extent the filmic devices underline the scientific achievements that have been made with the core drills.

3. Describe and analyze the graph. What does it say about global warming?

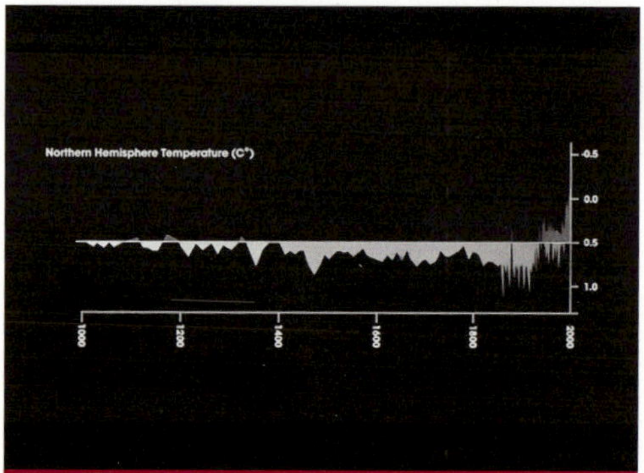

0:19:11

9 CO_2 LEVELS BACK 650,000 YEARS 0:19:34–0:23:51

1. Describe and analyze the two graphs. What do they show? What conclusions can be drawn from them?

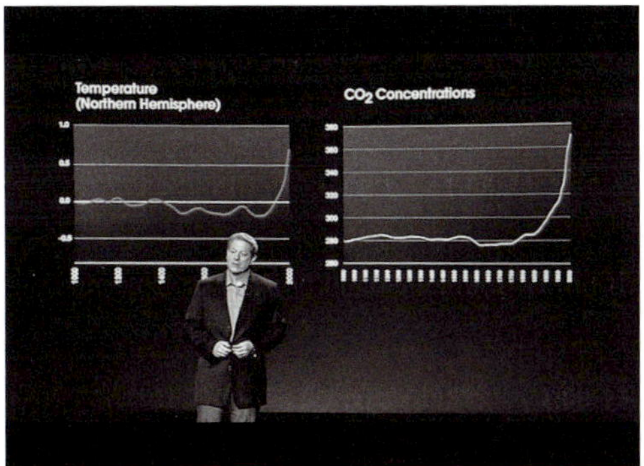

0:19:40

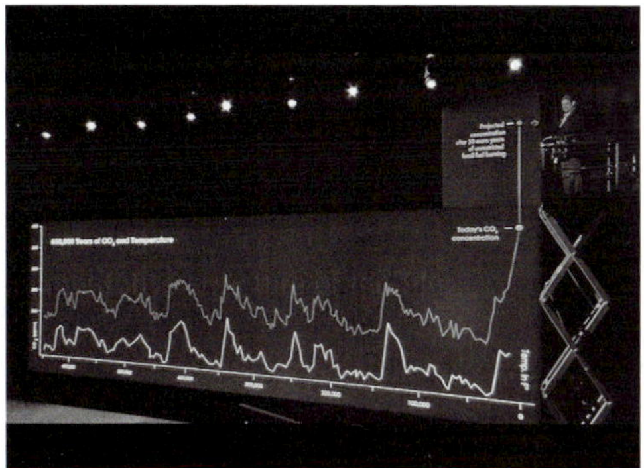
0:22:56

2. Explain how the present threat of CO_2 concentration in the atmosphere is made clear to the viewer. How is that threat underlined with the help of filmic devices?

3. Gore claims that global warming is more an ethical and moral than a political issue. Explain what he means and then comment on this statement.

10 ALBERT'S ACCIDENT 0:23:52–0:26:59

1. Analyze the function of this scene within the argumentative structure of the film. How is its significance made clear with the help of filmic devices?

2. Analyze to what extent the filmic devices help to point out Gore's personal dismay.

3. Explain the function of the sequence with the river [0:26:47–0:26:59] from the beginning at this stage of the film.

11 RISING TEMPERATURES 0:27:00–0:28:51

1. Summarize what Gore has to say about the world's temperature.

2. Analyze the argumentative structure and the filmic devices that are used in this passage to underline the effect that the rising temperatures have on America and the world.

3. Describe and analyze the graph in the still.

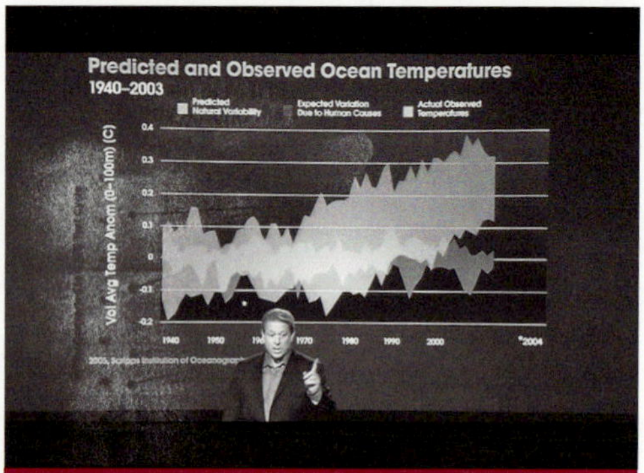

0:28:46

12 HURRICANES 0:28:52–0:32:51

1. Explain how from [0:28:52–0:29:55] the negative impact of temperature rise is underlined.

2. Explain how hurricane Katrina was able to grow in intensity after hitting Florida.

3. Analyze the filmic devices that are used to underline the tragedy that was caused by hurricane Katrina.

4. Summarize Gore's explanation as to how something like hurricane Katrina could have such a negative impact on a country like the USA.

5. Explain Sir Winston Churchill's statement of 12 November 1936, that "the era of procrastination, of half-measures, of soothing and baffling expedients, of delays, is coming to its close. In its place we are entering a period of consequences" and comment on it. In doing so also refer to other examples/situations in which it applies.

13 2000 ELECTION 0:32:52–0:35:20

1. Explain the function of the chapter "election 2000" at this stage of the movie.

2. Analyze the filmic devices that are used to point out that – in contrast to Bush – Gore would have been in control of the situation.

3. Summarize what you learn about the 2000 election in the USA and the US electoral system. Then read the information on p. 30 and explain how something like that could happen.

4. Summarize how Gore reacts to the outcome of the election (from [0:34:37–0:35:20]). Analyze the filmic devices that help to underline his reaction.

5. Analyze how – with the help of filmic devices – this chapter is linked with the next.

14 PRECIPITATION AND EVAPORATION 0:35:21–0:37:51

1. Summarize what Gore says about the consequences of global warming on precipitation.
2. Analyze the filmic devices that are used to emphasize the impact of global warming on precipitation.
3. Describe the map and explain why global warming leads to an increase in both precipitation and droughts.

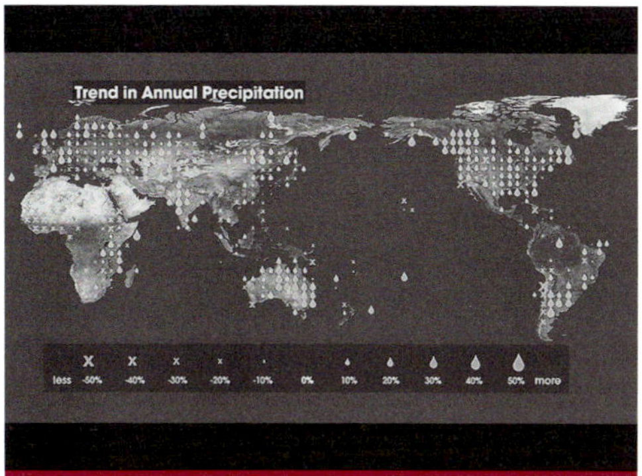

0:36:37

15 THE GORE FARM 0:37:52–0:40:03

1. Explain the function of this chapter within the argumentative structure of the film.
2. The viewer gets the impression that he is a private guest on Gore's farm. What film techniques are used to achieve this impression?
3. Describe Gore on the basis of this extract. What kind of person does he seem to be?

16 THE ARCTIC 0:40:04–0:44:00

1. On the basis of the still, explain how 40 % of the Arctic ice could melt in less than 40 years.
2. Summarize the consequences of global warming in the Arctic on the world.
3. Look up the expression "a canary in the coalmine" and explain its meaning in the context of this chapter.

0:42:56

4. Explain the consequences that the melting of the ice has on polar bears. Which filmic devices are used to underline the tragedy?

5. How does Gore manage to create suspense and maintain the viewers' interest at this stage of the film?

17 THE OCEAN CONVEYER 0:44:07–0:47:24

0:45:34

1. Explain why an average increase of temperature by 5 degrees will have such different effects at the equator and the poles.

2. Explain how the ocean conveyor works.

3. Explain the effect that a great ice dam breaking in America had on Europe after the last Ice Age. Why does Gore talk about this at this stage of the film?

18 RESISTANCE TO CHANGE 0:47:25–0:49:22

1. **Close Viewing**: Listen to the extract from the film and tick the correct statements. More than one statement is correct. Listen to the extract twice.

The USA is still by far the worst contributor to global warming.	
Gore is optimistic, because he can see that the attitude towards global warming in the USA is slowly changing and measures to prevent it are being taken.	
According to Bush, an environment-friendly policy would lead to an increase of unemployment in the USA.	
Gore is content, because the Bush administration plans to address the problem of global warming in the near future.	
Gore complains that the Bush administration can easily ignore the problem of global warming because US citizens are not really concerned about it.	

2. Describe Gore on the basis of this extract. What impression of him do you get? Take into consideration the filmic devices when discussing this.

3. In this film extract there are cross-cuts to the members of the Bush government. Explain the function of the cross-cuts within the film and summarize what these people have to say about Gore's position.

19 TROUBLING SIGNS 0:49:23–0:52:04

1. Summarize the impact that global warming has on us and the world.

2. Analyze how this impact is underlined with the help of filmic devices.

20 ANTARCTICA 0:52:05–0:54:58

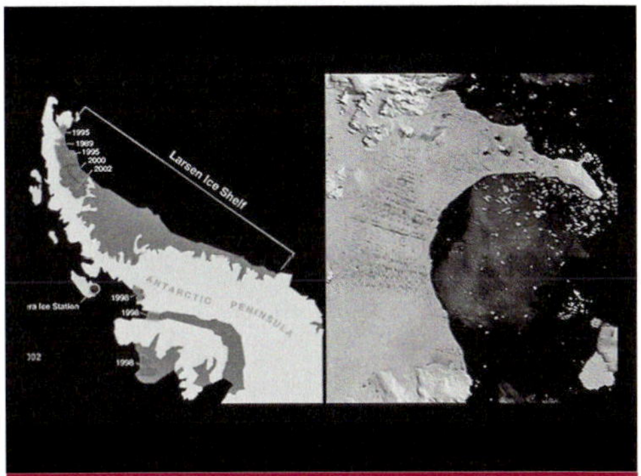

0:52:41

1. Explain what is going on at Larson Ice Shelf. In doing so, describe and analyze the still.

2. Explain the reasons why the shelf disappeared so rapidly, despite the scientists' predictions that it would last for at least another 100 years even with global warming.

3. Analyze how – with the help of filmic devices – the impact of the melting ice shelves on the environment is made clear to the viewer.

21 SEA-LEVEL RISE 0:54:59–0:58:46

1. Explain what is happening in Antarctica and in Greenland.

2. According to Blair, what has to be done because of the current ice melting? Explain why.

3. Analyze to what extent the filmic devices and Gore's comment help to underline the seriousness of the problem.

4. Explain Gore's appeal to the audience that "[they] should care about other things but terrorism as well" in the context of the film.

5. Do you agree that global warming is as serious a problem as terrorism? Discuss in class.

22 CHINA 0:58:47–1:00:56

1. Summarize what we learn about China and China's economy in this extract of the film.
2. Explain the function of this extract in the argumentative structure of the film.
3. Analyze how Gore's popularity is underlined with the help of filmic devices.

23 POPULATION EXPLOSION 1:00:57–1:02:37

1. Explain which three factors are leading to the "collision between our civilization and the earth".
2. Explain why Gore thinks this is a political issue.
3. Describe and analyze the still.

1:02:32

24 OLD HABITS + NEW TECHNOLOGY 1:02:38–1:06:43

1. **Close viewing:** Listen to the following extract from the film twice [1:02:38–1:05:03] and complete the table.

	Old technology	New technology	Examples
Warfare			–
Exploitation of the earth for sustenance			
Irrigation			

1. Explain why – according to Gore – it is difficult to combine old habits with new technology.
2. Analyze how – with the help of filmic devices and Gore's argumentation – this danger is made clear to the viewer.
3. Summarize the reasons for and the consequences of diverting rivers, using the example on the basis of the Aral Sea.

4. Analyze how – with the help of filmic devices – it is underlined that "making mistakes in our dealing with nature can have bigger consequences now."

5. Explain why the consequences of new technology are a political issue.

6. Summarize the frog cartoon [1:05:50–1:06:20] and explain its function within the argumentative structure of the film.

25 WORKING TOBACCO 1:06:44–1:09:12

1. Explain the function of this extract within the argumentative structure of the film.

26 IS THERE A CONTROVERSY? 1:09:13–1:10:51

1. Explain why there is a misconception about the consequences of global warming.

2. How does Gore try to convince the audience that the people questioning global warming are wrong?

27 SCIENCE FRAUD 1:10:52–1:13:53

1. Summarize the reasons why Gore reproaches the Bush government.

2. For background information read the information box and the newspaper article on p. 36.

3. The reproaches are not mentioned explicitly. Analyze how – with the help of filmic devices – the fact and seriousness of the fraud is made clear to the viewer.

4. Explain Sinclair's statement that "it is difficult to get a man to understand something when his salary depends upon his not understanding it" in reference to Philip Cooney and within the context of the film. Discuss this quotation with reference to other examples.

28 BALANCING THE ECOMOMY AND ENVIRONMENT 1:13:54–1:15:23

1. Explain why we do not have a choice between the economy and the environment.

29 CITY BY CITY 1:15:24–1:18:52

1. Characterize Gore on the basis of this extract. In doing so also point out to what extent the filmic devices help create this impression.

2. Describe and analyze the graph. In doing so explain why – according to Gore – the official American explanation that a choice between the economy and the environment cannot be made is ridiculous [1:17:24–1:18:52].

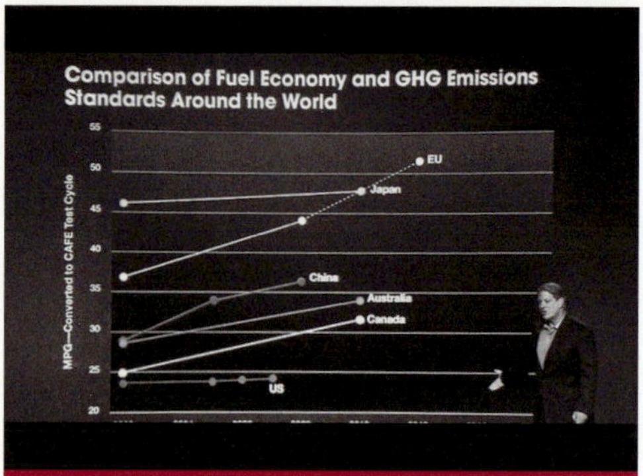

1:18:08

3. Explain the conclusion that Gore draws from US economic policy on the basis of this still.

30 THE SOLUTIONS ARE IN OUR HANDS 1:18:53–1:21:54

1. Discuss the statement that “we already possess the fundamental scientific, technical, and industrial know-how to solve the carbon and climate problems.”

2. What solutions to the problem does Gore mention?

3. Explain his statement that “political will is a renewable resource” and comment on it. Which message does Gore have for the American people.

4. Explain how everybody can help to do something about the problem. How is this underlined with the help of filmic devices?

31 ARE WE CAPABLE OF DOING GREAT THINGS? 1:21:26–1:23:11

1. Gore argues that humanity is capable of great things. How does he try to convince his audience that this is true?

2. What conclusion does Gore draw from the fact that the USA was the leading power to solve the problem about the hole in the ozone layer?

32 OUR ONLY HOME 1:23:12–1:25:58

1. Summarize Gore’s final appeal to the audience on the basis of the final photo. What is the function of this photo as a “final message”?

2. Analyze the function of the last pictures of the river in the argumentative structure of this film.

Questions on the Film

You are employed by "Planet Friendly", a climate change organization and have received an email from someone who would like to reduce their own carbon footprint but does not know how to calculate it. Moreover, they want to know all about the consequences of global warming and the impact of greenhouse gases in the atmosphere. Write to this person and make sure that you answer all their questions.

- **1** Is there any doubt as to whether global warming is occurring?
- **2** Is there any doubt that increasing levels of man-made CO_2 and other greenhouse gases are the main contributor to global warming?
- **3** Does the hole in the ozone layer cause global warming?
- **4** Is current global warming merely a part of long term temperature variations?
- **5** Does a record hot day count as evidence for global warming?
- **6** Does global warming mean less rain?
- **7** What does it mean to say that CO_2 acts as a greenhouse gas?
- **8** Is it true that electric vehicles do not contribute to the greenhouse effect?
- **9** Does hydrogen as a fuel contribute to the greenhouse effect?
- **10** Why can heat get in through the atmosphere, but not out through it?
- **11** What will cause a rise in sea levels?
- **12** How does recycling reduce global warming?
- **13** How does conserving water reduce global warming?
- **14** Do we need China and India to combat climate change?
- **15** Is it too late to repair the damage?
- **16** Can global warming be a good thing?
- **17** Does carbon offsetting remove the risk of global warming?
- **18** How can we tell if a product has produced a lot or little greenhouse gas before we buy it?

The US Electoral System and the 2000 Election

"I am Al Gore. I used to be the next president of the United States" [0:02:13–0:02:15]

Where the candidates stood in 2000 on the question of environmental issues

Al Gore

- Supported the Kyoto warming agreement.
- Supported a ban on off-shore drilling on undeveloped leases off the California and Florida coasts.
- Supported using $1 billion in federal funds to promote "smart growth" policies dealing with urban sprawl.
- Supported spending $2 billion over 10 years to create new parklands and open spaces: $1 billion in tax cuts to landowners who conserve property.
- Supported spending $1 billion for cities and states to control local parks.

George Bush

- Opposed the Kyoto global warming agreement.
- Believed that the threat of global warming should be addressed through new economic growth and efficiency.
- Supported increased state control over environmental policies.
- Supported oil exploration in Alaska's Arctic National Wildlife Refuge.
- Supported curbing the sulphur content of gasoline.

The Path to the US Presidency

20 January
President is sworn into office.

6 January
Results of the election in the Electoral College are declared.

Monday following the second Wednesday in December
Members of the Electoral College cast their vote.

Tuesday following the first Monday in November: ELECTION DAY
Registered voters elect the members of the Electoral College. The winner of the presidential election is usually known soon after.

ELECTORAL COLLEGE

- Consists of electors, who are elected by the US citizens.
- Numbers of electoral votes of each state is equal to the total number of members in Congress (in both the House of Representatives and the Senate): the higher the total number of representatives and senators from a state, the more electors will be there.
- In most states the candidate who wins the majority of popular votes in a state gets all of the state's electoral votes.

July/August
The presidential candidates of the parties are officially announced at the National Conventions.

January/March
Delegates who go to a party's national convention and vote for a presidential candidate are chosen by the states.

Nominee	**George W. Bush**	**Al Gore**
Party	Republican	Democratic
Home state	Texas	Tennessee
Running mate	Dick Cheney	Joe Lieberman
Popular vote in Florida	2,912,790	2,912,253
Percentage	48.85 %	48.84 %
Electoral vote in Florida	25	0

2000 Election Chronology

"The American people have spoken," said Bill Clinton shortly after election day. "It's too bad it's going to take a little while to determine what it was they had to say." The final result, which came five weeks later, put the Texas governor, George Bush, in the White House.

- **Tuesday, Nov. 7** Election Day. By early evening it is clear that it is the closest election ever and that the election hinges on Florida.
- **Wednesday, Nov. 8** Gore calls Bush at approximately 3 A.M. to concede, but retracts the concession shortly after, because of Bush's razor-slim lead and because Gore leads in the national popular count. This prompts an automatic recount.
- An unusual amount of votes for third-party candidates in some counties leads to disputes over the "butterfly ballots". A number of ballots in other counties are disqualified because the chad – the small piece of paper punched out of punch-card ballots – did not fully detach from the ballot.
- **Thursday, Nov. 9** Gore requests a hand recount of approximately 1.8 million ballots cast in Democratic strongholds.
- [***Until Saturday, Dec. 9*** *when the US Supreme Court votes 5–4 to stop the hand recounts, there are several lawsuits about whether hand recounts should be allowed or not and up to which date the results of the hand recounts must be included in the vote tally.*]
- **Friday, Nov. 10** Florida's automatic recount is completed. Bush leads but only by 327 votes.
- **Saturday, Nov. 18** With a tally of absentee ballots, Bush is ahead of Gore by 930 votes.
- **Sunday, Nov. 26** Harris certifies Bush as the winner of Florida's 25 electoral votes, with a 537-vote lead over Gore. Gore pledges to challenge certification in court. [...]
- The Florida Supreme Court denies Gore's appeal to immediately begin recounting ballots and rejects motion filed by some citizens who questioned the integrity of the "butterfly ballot".

Popular Vote

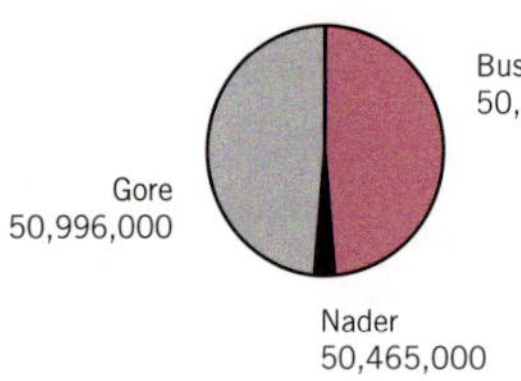

Electoral Vote

2 *hinge on sth.* depend completely on sth.
3 *concede (v.), (n = concession)* admit defeat
4 *retract sth.* say that you did not mean what you said before
7 *third-party candidates* other presidential candidates who usually get only few votes
8 *butterfly ballot* ballot (= a piece of paper on which you make a private vote) which has names on the left and right and punch holes in the centre
10 *punch-card ballots* ballot in which a hole is punched next to a candidate's name
10 *detach sth.* separate sth.
17 *vote tally* record of how many votes a candidate has
20 *absentee ballot* postal vote
22 *Katherine Harris* Republican Secretary of State in Florida in 2000
23 *pledge sth.* promise sth.
26 *file a motion* make a formal proposal in court

- **Tuesday, Dec. 12** The US Supreme Court rules in Bush v. Gore 7–2 to reverse the Florida Supreme Court, which had ordered manual recounts in certain counties. The Court contends that the recount was not treating all ballots equally, and was thus a violation of the Constitution's equal protection and due process guarantees. The Supreme Court of Florida would be required to set up new voting standards and carry them out in a recount. [...] The decision generates enormous controversy. Those objecting to the ruling assert that the Supreme Court, and not the electorate, has effectively determined the outcome of the presidential election. [...]
- Gore concedes, and Bush accepts the presidency.
- **Monday, Dec. 18** Electoral College representatives meet in state capitals and cast votes to select president. [...]
- **Saturday, Jan. 20** George W. Bush sworn in as 43rd president of the United States

From: the website of Infoplease, 2001. Information Please ® Database,

30 *contend* argue
31 *Constitution's equal protection and due process guarantees* all ballots must be treated equally, as laid down in the American Constitution
35 *assert* to state firmly that sth. is true

■ **1** Discuss Clinton's statement that it took "a little while to determine what [the American people] had to say during the 2000 election". Do you think that the American people were carefully listened to? Explain your opinion with reference to the election chronology and the US electoral system.

■ **2** After the 2000 US election a reform of the electoral system was discussed. Do you consider that this is necessary? Discuss this question in class.

■ **3** Project:
Find information on other electoral systems (e.g. the UK or Germany) and present them to the class comparing them to the US system. These questions may help you:
- How are the seats of the representatives (i.e. the House of Representatives, the Senate, the "Bundestag", Parliament) distributed among the different parties?
- How is the American President / the German Chancellor / Prime Minister chosen?
- What power do the Monarch and the Prime Minister in the UK, the President and the Chancellor in Germany, and the American President have?

Discuss advantages and disadvantages of the different systems.

The Kyoto Protocol

> The Kyoto Protocol is an international agreement on climate change. It aims to delay climate change by reducing the total greenhouse gas emissions of developed countries (and countries with economies in transition).

> It was adopted in Kyoto, Japan, on 11 December 1997 and entered into force in February 2005 after Russia signed it. (It had to be signed by 55 countries – including those responsible for at least 55 % of the developed world's CO_2 emissions – before it could enter into force).

> As the industrialized nations have the major responsibility for the current high levels of greenhouse gases in the atmosphere, the protocol places heavier burdens on these nations than on developing nations.

> It sets legally binding targets for the greenhouse gas emissions of the countries that have ratified it for the period 2008–2012. Those countries that do not comply with their targets have to take responsibility for excess emissions.

> Different countries have different targets: From 8 % below to 10 % above the 1990 level. (8 % below the 1990 level for the EU).

> Only countries that ratify the Kyoto Protocol are bound to it.

> For countries that cannot achieve their targets by reducing greenhouse gas emissions at home there are so-called "flexibility mechanisms", e.g. they can "buy emissions" from countries that have reduced their emissions below their targets or they can make up for higher emissions by increasing and maintaining carbon sinks (e.g. planting forests that help to remove greenhouse gases from the atmosphere.)

> The Kyoto Protocol encourages the following measures to reduce greenhouse gas emissions:
– Enhancement of energy efficiency
– Protection of sinks and reservoirs of greenhouse gases
– Promotion of afforestation and reforestation
– Promotion of environmentally friendly forms of agriculture
– Research on, development of and increased use of new and renewable forms of energy and of CO_2 sequestration technologies
– Progressive reduction of all tax exemptions and subsidies in all greenhouse gas emitting industries
– Reduction of greenhouse gas emissions in the transport sector

1 Read the information about the Kyoto Protocol on the previous page and then the arguments for and against signing the Kyoto Protocol below. Discuss which side is more convincing to you. To find out more about the pros and cons of the Kyoto Protocol you can also read:

- *Bush on Climate Change* (p. 45)
- *The Cancún Summit on Climate Change in 2010* (p. 40).

Arguments for signing the protocol
– It helps to reduce greenhouse gases. – It is an essential step in slowing down or reversing global warming. – It makes immediate multinational collaboration possible. – It forces the industrialized nations that are responsible for the concentration of greenhouse gases to take greater responsibility than the developing nations.

Arguments against signing the protocol
The Kyoto Protocol demands too much: – The signing of the treaty would harm the US economy, leading to economic losses of $400 billion and costing 4.9 million jobs. – It is not acceptable to exempt the developing nations.
The Kyoto Protocol achieves too little: – Planting forests (which many nations rely on) is not effective; instead it will increase CO_2 for the first ten years. – If the need for fossil fuels goes down in the industrialized nations, the prices will decrease and they will become more affordable for the developing nations; this will simply shift the emissions from one place to another. – It focuses too much on greenhouse gases without taking other factors like population growth and other issues into account.

The Case of Philip A. Cooney

Philip A. Cooney is mentioned in the film as changing scientific findings to make it appear that the threat of global warming was exaggerated. This is the newspaper article that led to Cooney's resignation.

A White House official who once led the oil industry's fight against limits on greenhouse gases has repeatedly edited government climate reports in ways that play down links between such emissions and global warming, according to internal documents.

In handwritten notes on drafts of several reports issued in 2002 and 2003, the official, Philip A. Cooney, removed or adjusted descriptions of climate research that government scientists and their supervisors, including some senior Bush administration officials, had already approved. In many cases, the changes appeared in the final reports.

The dozens of changes, while sometimes as subtle as the insertion of the phrase "significant and fundamental" before the word "uncertainties," tend to produce an air of doubt about findings that most climate experts say are robust.

Mr. Cooney is chief of staff for the White House Council on Environmental Quality, the office that helps devise and promote administration policies on environmental issues.

Before going to the White House in 2001, he was the "climate team leader" and a lobbyist at the American Petroleum Institute, the largest trade group representing the interests of the oil industry. A lawyer with a bachelor's degree in economics, he has no scientific training.

The documents were obtained by The New York Times from the Government Accountability Project, a nonprofit legal-assistance group for government whistle-blowers.

The project is representing Rick S. Piltz, who resigned in March as a senior associate in the office that coordinates government climate research. That office, now called the Climate Change Science Program, issued the documents that Mr. Cooney edited.

A White House spokeswoman, Michele St. Martin, said yesterday that Mr. Cooney would not be available to comment. "We don't put Phil Cooney on the record," Ms. St. Martin said. "He's not a cleared spokesman."

In one instance in an October 2002 draft of a regularly published summary of government climate research, "Our Changing Planet," Mr. Cooney amplified the sense of uncertainty by adding the word "extremely" to this sentence: "The attribution of the causes of biological and ecological changes to climate change or variability is extremely difficult."

In a section on the need for research into how warming might change water availability and flooding, he crossed out a paragraph describing the projected reduction of mountain glaciers and snowpack. His note in the

23 *whistle-blower* person who tells the public or people in authority about dishonest or illegal behavior

30 *cleared spokesman* person who has official permission to speak with the press

INFO

Philip A. Cooney

- US oil industry lobbyist.
- He became chief of the White House Council on Environmental Quality in 2001 without having any scientific background.
- He deleted or changed scientific findings in federal reports about global warming and its imminent dangers during the next four years.
- At the White House he routinely criticized climate-change research.
- Cooney left his White House position in 2005, after *The New York Times* wrote an exposé of the disinformation he had been involved in.
- The next day he was hired by Exxon Mobil to become its Corporate Issues Manager.

margins explained that this was "straying from research strategy into speculative findings/musings."

Other White House officials said the changes made by Mr. Cooney were part of the normal interagency review that takes place on all documents related to global environmental change. Robert Hopkins, a spokesman for the White House Office of Science and Technology Policy, noted that one of the reports Mr. Cooney worked on, the administration's 10-year plan for climate research, was endorsed by the National Academy of Sciences. And Myron Ebell, who has long campaigned against limits on greenhouse gases as director of climate policy at the Competitive Enterprise Institute, a libertarian group, said such editing was necessary for "consistency" in meshing programs with policy.

But critics said that while all administrations routinely vetted government reports, scientific content in such reports should be reviewed by scientists. Climate experts and representatives of environmental groups, when shown examples of the revisions, said they illustrated the significant if largely invisible influence of Mr. Cooney and other White House officials with ties to energy industries that have long fought greenhouse-gas restrictions.

In a memorandum sent last week to the top officials dealing with climate change at a dozen agencies, Mr. Piltz said the White House editing and other actions threatened to taint the government's $1.8 billion-a-year effort to clarify the causes and consequences of climate change.

"Each administration has a policy position on climate change," Mr. Piltz wrote. "But I have not seen a situation like the one that has developed under this administration during the past four years, in which politicization by the White House has fed back directly into the science

48 *endorse sth.* express formal support or approval for sth.
52 *mesh sth.* make sure that two things/attitudes fit together
53 *vet sth.* check sth. (e.g. reports or speeches)
62 *taint sth.* make sth. look bad

program in such a way as to undermine the credibility and integrity of the program."

A senior Environmental Protection Agency scientist who works on climate questions said the White House environmental council, where Mr. Cooney works, had offered valuable suggestions on reports from time to time. But the scientist, who spoke on the condition of anonymity because all agency employees are forbidden to speak with reporters without clearance, said the kinds of changes made by Mr. Cooney had damaged morale. "I have colleagues in other agencies who express the same view, that it has somewhat of a chilling effect and has created a sense of frustration," he said.

Efforts by the Bush administration to highlight uncertainties in science pointing to human-caused warming have put the United States at odds with other nations and with scientific groups at home.

Prime Minister Tony Blair of Britain, who met with President Bush at the White House yesterday, has been trying to persuade him to intensify United States efforts to curb greenhouse gases. Mr. Bush has called only for voluntary measures to slow growth in emissions through 2012.

Yesterday, saying their goal was to influence that meeting, the scientific academies of 11 countries, including those of the United States and Britain, released a joint letter saying, "The scientific understanding of climate change is now sufficiently clear to justify nations taking prompt action."

The American Petroleum Institute, where Mr. Cooney worked before going to the White House, has long taken a sharply different view. Starting with the negotiations leading to the Kyoto Protocol climate treaty in 1997, it has promoted the idea that lingering uncertainties in climate science justify delaying restrictions on emissions of carbon dioxide and other heat-trapping smokestack and tailpipe gases.

On learning of the White House revisions, representatives of some environmental groups said the effort to amplify uncertainties in the science was clearly intended to delay consideration of curbs on the gases, which remain an unavoidable byproduct of burning oil and coal.

"They've got three more years, and the only way to control this issue and do nothing about it is to muddy the science," said Eileen Claussen, the president of the Pew Center on Global Climate Change, a private group that has enlisted businesses in programs cutting emissions.

Mr. Cooney's alterations can cause clear shifts in meaning. For example, a sentence in the October 2002 draft of "Our Changing Planet" originally read, "Many scientific observations indicate that the Earth is undergoing a period of relatively rapid change." In a neat, compact hand, Mr. Cooney modified the sentence to read, "Many scientific observations point to the conclusion that the Earth may be undergoing a period of relatively rapid change."

From: A. Revkin, "Bush Aide Softened Greenhouse Gas Links to Global Warming", The New York Times, *8 June 2005. © 2011 The New York Times. All rights reserved.*

97 *smokestack* a tall chimney at a factory
97 *tailpipe* a pipe on a vehicle or machine through which gas passes
99 *amplify* increase the effect of sth.
100 *curb* a limit on sth. in order to prevent it from having a harmful effect
103 *muddy sth. (infml)* make sth. more complicated and confusing than it was before

■ **1** The publication of this newspaper article led to Cooney's resignation from office. Summarize what Cooney was accused of.

■ **2** Describe the consequences of this affair for the American government.

■ **3** Explain why the American Petrolium Institute allegedly approved of Cooney's behavior in the White House.

■ **4** Analyze how some White House officials tried to defend Cooney.

■ **5** Analyze how the writer makes his view of Clooney clear to the readers without being explicit.

■ **6** Look at the exercises in the *While-watching Activities* and analyze the corresponding passage in the film (cf. chapter "Science Fraud").

■ **7** Comment on Philip Cooney's behavior.

The Cancún Summit on Climate Change in 2010

The 2010 United Nations Climate Change Conference was held in Cancún, Mexico, from 29 November to 10 December 2010. The conference served to continue action on the Kyoto Protocol. Below is a list of the main terms of the deal reached at the Cancún.

Cancún climate agreements at a glance

Cutting carbon emissions

Scores of rich countries made pledges over the past year to cut their greenhouse gas emissions by 2020 under the Copenhagen accord but they were not incorporated in the official UN process. Cancún now formally puts those pledges into UN documentation, although they may increase or decrease in future. For the first time, developing countries also agreed to look at how they can cut emissions in the future – but did not make specific pledges.

Crucially however, none of the cuts are legally binding, and analysis suggests the pledges would lead to a 3.2C rise in temperatures – far higher than the 2C generally considered to be a level of "safe" warming.

Climate aid

A new climate green fund was agreed at Cancún to transfer money from the developed to developing world to tackle the impacts of climate change. Poorer countries saw this as a success because they will outnumber rich countries on a 'transitional committee' for the fund, which is due to be set up in 2011. But no figure was put on how much money will go into it.

Separately, ministers repeated their political promise made last year at Copenhagen to raise $100bn (£63bn) in climate aid by 2020, starting with $30bn (£19bn) by 2012 for "fast track" financing. This headline-grabbing promise, however, is not part of the UN process and is merely an aspiration of rich countries.

Forests

Formal backing was given for the UN's deforestation scheme, Redd (reducing emissions from deforestation and degradation), under which rich countries pay poorer nations not to chop down forests and so lock away carbon emissions. But details on when and exactly what form the scheme will take – particularly whether developed countries will be able to use it to "offset" their emissions rather than make cuts at home – are still vague.

Kyoto protocol

Decisions on the future of the Kyoto protocol, the current international treaty binding rich countries to cut emissions, were effectively deferred until South Africa next year. Whether countries will sign up for a second "commitment period" to cuts beyond 2012 remains to be seen.

2 *make pledges* make promises
3 *the Copenhagen accord* the agreement from the previous year's summit in Copenhagen
14 *tackle the impacts of sth.* deal with the effects of sth.
21 *headline-grabbing* that is so interesting that the newspapers write about it on the first pages
25 *deforestation scheme* agreement about how many forests can be cut down
34 *defer sth.* delay sth.
36 *commitment period* a promise to do something over a period of time

In addition, decisions on the role that the protocol will play in an ultimate future legal document that binds the world's countries to emissions cuts – the "holy grail" of the UN negotiations – were delayed.

Technology transfer

The idea of transferring knowledge of clean technology between countries was backed at Cancún. A technology executive committee and a climate technology centre and network are to be set up, but there are no details on the money, where they will be based, when or by whom.

Inspections

Countries agreed to the principle of having their emissions cuts inspected. Such "monitoring, reporting and verification" will depend on the size of the country's economy, though who will carry out the inspections – the country itself, the UN or another body – was not specified.

42 *back sth.* support sth.

From: Adam Vaughan, Guardian, *13 December 2010.*

Cancún agreement rescues UN credibility but falls short of saving planet

The modest deal wrangled out by the 200 countries meeting at the Mexican resort of Cancún may have done more to save a dysfunctional UN negotiating process from collapse than protect the planet against climate change, analysts said today.

The agreement produced in the early hours of Saturday reinforces the promise made by rich countries last year to mobilize billions for a green climate fund to help poor countries defend themselves against climate damage. [...]

Cancún also produced a victory for forest campaigners who were looking to the talks to produce a system of incentives to prevent the destruction of tropical rainforests in countries such as Brazil, Congo and Indonesia. Under the deal, developing countries will receive aid for not burning or logging forests. Deforestation produces about 15% of the world's carbon emissions. [...]

Negotiators, clean-energy business associations and campaign groups warned that Cancún's most significant result was putting off the tough decisions until next year's UN summit in South Africa.

"The outcome wasn't enough to save the planet," said Alden Meyer of the Union of Concerned Scientists. "But it did restore the credibility of the United Nations as a forum where progress can be made."

The Global Wind Energy Council said Cancún was only counted a success because of the extremely low expectations going into the talks. "None of the fundamental political, legal and architectural issues that still must be resolved in order to establish an effective global climate regime have been solved," it said.

1 *wrangle out a deal* come to an agreement about what to do after long and difficult argument
3 *UN negotiating process* way that decisions are reached when each side compromises on something
10 *incentive* something that encourages people to take new initiatives
13 *log forests* cut down trees

> *"If, from here, we send the Kyoto Protocol to the rubbish bin, we are responsible for ecocide and genocide, because we will be sending many people to their death."*
>
> **Evo Morales**, President of Bolivia,
> at the UN conference on climate change in Cancún, Mexico

Michael Levi, a fellow at the Council on Foreign Relations, warned that the failure to resolve difficult issues at Cancún – especially over the future of the Kyoto protocol – makes the risks even higher next year.

He wrote on his blog: "The Cancún result puts the dispute to next year's talks. But that solution will not be available again: the current Kyoto commitments expire at the end of 2012, making the next UN conference the last practical opportunity to seal a new set of Kyoto pledges."

But negotiators did not have many options. After the failure of the Copenhagen summit last year, a breakdown at Cancún would have condemned the 20-year climate negotiations, Connie Hedegaard, the European Union's climate commissioner, told reporters on Saturday.

In the run-up to Cancún, negotiators acknowledged there was no prospect of reaching a new treaty. They hoped instead for progress on the "building blocks" to a deal, such as detailed agreements on climate finance, preventing deforestation, enabling technology transfer and accounting for emissions cuts by emerging economies such as China and India.

However, even those modest ambitions were put in jeopardy when Japan and then Russia announced they would not sign on to a second term of the Kyoto protocol unless the world's big emitters, China and the US, were also legally bound to action.

Campaign groups such as Greenpeace also blamed the US for taking a hard line at the talks – partly for fear of being accused of giving up too much to China by Republicans at home.

Despite those tensions, however, America and China avoided the mood of confrontation that undermined the talks at Copenhagen last year.

From: Suzanne Goldberg, Guardian, *12 December 2010.*

44 *put in jeopardy* put sth. in danger
47 *bind sb. legally to action* make sb. take action

1 Comment on the President of Bolivia's quote on the importance of the summit at Cancún.

2 Read the two texts. Then get into two groups. One group collects all the arguments for why the summit at Cancún was a success. The other group collects all the arguments for why the summit was not a success and "falls short of saving the planet". After collecting the arguments, get together with a person from the other group and discuss the pros and cons of the summit.

3 Write a comment on the summit, in which you express your opinion on it. Do not forget to give reasons for your position.

An Inconvenient Truth about Al Gore

People have not only criticized Gore's movie, but also his lifestyle, claiming that he does not live up to the changes he urges people to make in their own lives. This article examines some of his alleged hypocrisy.

Al Gore has spoken. The world must embrace a "carbon-neutral lifestyle." To do otherwise will result in a cataclysmic catastrophe. "Humanity is sitting on a ticking time bomb," warns the website for his film, *An Inconvenient Truth*. "We have just 10 years to avert a major catastrophe that could send our entire planet into a tailspin."

Graciously, Gore tells consumers how to change their lives to curb their carbon-gobbling ways: Switch to compact fluorescent light bulbs, use a clothesline, drive a hybrid, use renewable energy, dramatically cut back on consumption. Better still, responsible global citizens can follow Gore's example, because, as he readily points out in his speeches, he lives a "carbon-neutral lifestyle." But if Al Gore is the world's role model for ecology, the planet is doomed.

For someone who says the sky is falling, he does very little. He says he recycles and drives a hybrid. And he claims he uses renewable energy credits to offset the pollution he produces when using a private jet to promote his film. (In reality, Paramount Classics, the film's distributor, pays this.)

Public records reveal that as Gore lectures Americans on excessive consumption, he and his wife Tipper live in two properties: a 10,000-square-foot, 20-room, eight-bathroom home in Nashville, and a 4,000-square-foot home in Arlington, Va. (He also has a third home in Carthage, Tenn.) For someone rallying the planet to pursue a path of extreme personal sacrifice, Gore requires little from himself.

Then there is the troubling matter of his energy use. In the Washington, D.C., area, utility companies offer wind energy as an alternative to traditional energy. In Nashville, similar programs exist. Utility customers must simply pay a few extra pennies per kilowatt hour, and they can continue living their carbon-neutral lifestyles knowing that they are supporting wind energy. Plenty of businesses and institutions have signed up. Even the Bush administration is using green energy for some federal office buildings, as are thousands of area residents. But according to public records, there is no evidence that Gore has signed up to use green energy in either of his large residences. When contacted Wednesday, Gore's office confirmed as much but said the Gores were looking into making the switch at both homes. Talk about inconvenient truths. [...]

Gore has held these apocalyptic views about the environment for some time. So why, then, didn't Gore dump his family's large stock holdings in Occidental (Oxy) Petroleum? As executor of his family's

7 *gobble* eat sth. very quickly
7 *compact fluorescent light bulb* Energiesparlampe
8 *clothesline* line on which clothes are dried (rather than a dryer)
8 *hybrid* ['haɪbrɪd] vehicle that uses two or more distinct power sources to move the vehicle. The term most commonly refers to hybrid electric vehicles (HEVs), which combine an internal combustion engine and one or more electric motors.
14 *renewable energy credits* certificates issued by a government agency to a power company which generates environmentally friendly electricity.
15 *offset sth.* act to counteract the effect of sth. so that the situation remains the same
21 *Va.* Virgina
22 *Tenn.* Tennessee
25 *utility company* Versorgungsunternehmen
38 *dump stock holdings* give up shares in a company

trust, over the years Gore has controlled hundreds of thousands of dollars in Oxy stock. Oxy has been mired in controversy over oil drilling in ecologically sensitive areas. [...]

The issue here is not simply Gore's hypocrisy; it's a question of credibility. If he genuinely believes the apocalyptic vision he has put forth and calls for radical changes in the way other people live, why hasn't he made any radical change in his life? Giving up the zinc mine or one of his homes is not asking much, given that he wants the rest of us to radically change our lives.

41 *be mired* be stuck in a bad situation and to be unable to get out

From: Peter Schweizer, "Gore Isn't quite as Green as He's Led the World to Believe", USA Today, *12 July 2006. © 2011 USA Today, a division of Gannett Co. Inc.*

■ **1** Collect all the information in the article that contrasts Gore's desire for everyone to become environmentally friendly and his own behavior.

Things he urges people to do to be environmentally friendly	Things he does that show he is not environmentally friendly

■ **2** Analyze the text, showing how the writer's negative opinion about Gore is made clear to the reader by means of rhetorical devices, the structure of the text and the choice of words.

■ **3** Describe and analyze the cartoon below. What do you think is the cartoonist's opinion about Gore's credibility?

■ **4** Write a letter to the producers of the film in which you express your opinion about Gore's lifestyle.

"Al Gore's going to Oslo, Norway, to accept the Nobel Peace Prize for his courageous efforts to reduce carbon dioxide emissions."

Bush on Climate Change

This test is a shortened version of President Bush's first speech on climate change, delivered on 11 June 2001.

Good morning. I've just met with senior members of my administration who are working to develop an effective and science-based approach to addressing the important issues of global climate change.

This is an issue that I know is very important to the nations of Europe, which I will be visiting for the first time as President. The earth's well-being is also an issue important to America. And it's an issue that should be important to every nation in every part of our world.

The issue of climate change respects no border. Its effects cannot be reined in by an army nor advanced by any ideology. Climate change, with its potential to impact every corner of the world, is an issue that must be addressed by the world.

The Kyoto Protocol was fatally flawed in fundamental ways. But the process used to bring nations together to discuss our joint response to climate change is an important one. That is why I am today committing the United States of America to work within the United Nations framework and elsewhere to develop with our friends and allies and nations throughout the world an effective and science-based response to the issue of global warming. [...]

First, we know the surface temperature of the earth is warming. It has risen by 6 degrees Celsius over the past 100 years. There was a warming trend from the 1890s to the 1940s. Cooling from the 1940s to the 1970s. And then sharply rising temperatures from the 1970s to today. There is a natural greenhouse effect that contributes to warming. Greenhouse gases trap heat, and thus warm the earth because they prevent a significant proportion of infrared radiation from escaping into space. Concentration of greenhouse gases, especially CO_2, have increased substantially since the beginning of the industrial revolution. And the National Academy of Sciences indicate that the increase is due in large part to human activity.

Yet, the Academy's report tells us that we do not know how much effect natural fluctuations in climate may have had on warming. We do not know how much our climate could, or will change in the future. We do not know how fast change will occur, or even how some of our actions could impact it.

[...] And, finally, no one can say with any certainty what constitutes a dangerous level of warming, and therefore what level must be avoided.

The policy challenge is to act in a serious and sensible way, given the limits of our knowledge. While scientific uncertainties remain, we can begin now to address the factors that contribute to climate change.

There are only two ways to stabilize concentration of greenhouse gases. One is to avoid emitting them in the first place; the other is to try

9 *rein sth. in* start to control sth. more strictly
12 *be flawed* to be spoiled by having mistakes

to capture them after they're created. And there are problems with both approaches. We're making great progress through technology, but have not yet developed cost-effective ways to capture carbon emissions at their source; although there is some promising work that is being done.

And a growing population requires more energy to heat and cool our homes, more gas to drive our cars. Even though we're making progress on conservation and energy efficiency and have significantly reduced the amount of carbon emissions per unit of GDP.

Our country, the United States is the world's largest emitter of manmade greenhouse gases. We account for almost 20 percent of the world's man-made greenhouse emissions. We also account for about one-quarter of the world's economic output. We recognize the responsibility to reduce our emissions. We also recognize the other part of the story – that the rest of the world emits 80 percent of all greenhouse gases. And many of those emissions come from developing countries.

This is a challenge that requires a 100 percent effort; ours, and the rest of the world's. The world's second-largest emitter of greenhouse gases is China. Yet, China was entirely exempted from the requirements of the Kyoto Protocol.

India and Germany are among the top emitters. Yet, India was also exempt from Kyoto. These and other developing countries that are experiencing rapid growth face challenges in reducing their emissions without harming their economies. We want to work cooperatively with these countries in their efforts to reduce greenhouse emissions and maintain economic growth.

Kyoto also failed to address two major pollutants that have an impact on warming: black soot and tropospheric ozone. Both are proven health hazards. Reducing both would not only address climate change, but also dramatically improve people's health.

Kyoto is, in many ways, unrealistic. Many countries cannot meet their Kyoto targets. The targets themselves were arbitrary and not based upon science. For America, complying with those mandates would have a negative economic impact, with layoffs of workers and price increases for consumers. And when you evaluate all these flaws, most reasonable people will understand that it's not sound public policy.

That's why 95 members of the United States Senate expressed a reluctance to endorse such an approach. Yet, America's unwillingness to embrace a flawed treaty should not be read by our friends and allies as any abdication of responsibility. To the contrary, my administration is committed to a leadership role on the issue of climate change.

We recognize our responsibility and will meet it – at home, in our hemisphere, and in the world. My Cabinet-level working group on climate change is recommending a number of initial steps, and will continue to work on additional ideas. The working group proposes the United States help lead the way by advancing the science on climate change, advancing the technology to monitor and reduce greenhouse

68 *black soot* black powder that is produced when sth. is burned
69 *hazard* risk
73 *comply with sth.* obey regulations concerning sth.
78 *endorse sth.* express formal support of sth.
80 *abdication (fml)* refusal to take the responsibility for sth.

gases, and creating partnerships within our hemisphere and beyond to monitor and measure and mitigate emissions.

I also call on Congress to work with my administration to achieve the significant emission reductions made possible by implementing the clean energy technologies proposed in our energy plan. Our working group study has made it clear that we need to know a lot more.

[...] Even with the best science, even with the best technology, we all know the United States cannot solve this global problem alone. We're building partnerships within the Western Hemisphere and with other like-minded countries. [...]

I've asked Secretary Powell and Administrator Whitman to ensure they actively work with friends and allies to explore common approaches to climate change consistent with these principles. Each step we take will increase our knowledge. We will act, learn, and act again, adjusting our approaches as science advances and technology evolves.

Our administration will be creative. We're committed to protecting our environment and improving our economy, to acting at home and working in concert with the world. This is an administration that will make commitments we can keep, and keep the commitments that we make.

I look forward to continued discussions with our friends and allies about this important issue.

Thank you for coming.

■ 1 *Reading for gist*

Bush's speech is about ...

a. the plans of the Bush administration to sign the Kyoto Protocol after further negotiations with China, India and Germany.
b. the reasons why the Americans have not signed the Kyoto Protocol despite their willingness to work together with other nations of the world on the issue of climate change.
c. Bush's opinion that the reason for global warming is just the effect of natural fluctuations in climate and that therefore people do not have to be worried.
d. the enormous costs of research to develop improved technology for monitoring greenhouse gas emissions and the negative impact that they have on the American economy.
e. Bush's belief that because of technical progress greenhouse gas emissions can be reduced in the near future.

2 *Reading for detail*
Write down the letters of those statements that reflect Bush's opinion about the Kyoto Protocol correctly.

a. Countries like India and China do not have to reduce their greenhouse gas emissions.
b. Germany emits more greenhouse gases than the USA.
c. As greenhouse gases are not the only major pollutants, the Kyoto Protocol also regulates the emissions of ozone and black sooth.
d. The compliance of the Kyoto targets would lead to an increase of unemployment and of prices in the USA.
e. The Kyoto Protocol is not fair. Although the USA emit about 20 % of the world's man-made greenhouse gases, they also account for 25 % of the world's economic output. And these two aspects are closely connected.
f. The Kyoto targets were agreed upon after thorough research by scientists.
g. Despite the mistakes that the Kyoto Protocol contains, it started the process of bringing nations together and discussing problems that affect the whole world.
h. The Bush administration wants to help the developing countries to contribute to the reduction of greenhouse gas emissions without sacrificing economic growth.
i. The fact that we neither know, if the rising temperatures are only the effect of natural fluctuations in temperature nor if our actions can impact them, proves that the Kyoto Protocol is flawed.

3 *Reading for detail*
Despite his reluctance to sign the Kyoto Protocol, Bush claims that his "administration is committed to a leadership role on the issue of climate change" (ll. 80–81). Write down the letters of those statements that explain what measures he wants to take in order to meet the USA's responsibility.

a. The USA initiates the creation of partnerships within the Northern hemisphere and beyond to measure emissions.
b. They plan to re-evaluate the measures that they take whenever science advances.
c. The Bush administration wants to work together with Congress to reduce greenhouse gas emissions effectively by implementing clean energy technologies.
d. The USA wants to rely on clean energy technologies to reduce greenhouse gas emissions.
e. The Bush administration does not only want to concentrate on the reduction of greenhouse gas emissions.
f. The reduction of greenhouse gas emissions is so important that it must be achieved even if it inhibits further economic growth in America and in other countries of the world.

4 Analyze Bush's speech. In doing so find out who he addresses in his speech and how he tries to convince his audience of his ideas.

5 Write a letter to George W. Bush, in which you comment on his speech and his plans to stop global warming taking into account the information you have learned from the film *An Inconvenient Truth*.

The Reception of the Film

In the year from its release in May 2006 *An Inconvenient Truth*:
- became the third-highest grossing documentary ever in the USA, making more than $23 million.
- earned $49 million at the box office worldwide.
- won an Oscar for Best Documentary.

Below are two newspaper articles looking at the movie.

Warning of Calamities and Hoping for a Change in *An Inconvenient Truth*

An Inconvenient Truth, Davis Guggenheim's new documentary about the dangers of climate change, is a film that should never have been made. It is, after all, the job of political leaders and policymakers to protect against possible future calamities, to respond to the findings of science and to persuade the public that action must be taken to protect the common interest.

But when this does not happen – and it is hardly a partisan statement to observe that, in the case of global warming, it hasn't – others must take up the responsibility: filmmakers, activists, scientists, even retired politicians. That *An Inconvenient Truth* should not have to exist is a reason to be grateful that it does.

Appearances to the contrary, Mr. Guggenheim's movie is not really about Al Gore. It consists mainly of a multimedia presentation on climate change that Mr. Gore has given many times over the last few years, interspersed with interviews and Mr. Gore's voice-over reflections on his life in and out of politics. His presence is, in some ways, a distraction, since it guarantees that *An Inconvenient Truth* will become fodder for the cynical, ideologically facile sniping that often passes for political discourse these days. But really, the idea that worrying about the effect of carbon-dioxide emissions on the world's climate makes you some kind of liberal kook is as tired as the image of Mr. Gore as a stiff, humorless speaker, someone to make fun of rather than take seriously.

In any case, Mr. Gore has long since proven to be a deft self-satirist. (He recently told a moderator at a Cannes Film Festival news conference to address him as "your Adequacy.") He makes a few jokes to leaven the grim gist of *An Inconvenient Truth*, and some of them are funny, in the style of a college lecturer's attempts to keep the attention of his captive audience. Indeed, his onstage manner – pacing back and forth, fiddling with gadgets, gesturing for emphasis – is more a professor's than a politician's. If he were not the man who, in his own formulation "used to be the next president of the United States of America," he might have

17 *become fodder* be a target for criticism
18 *ideologically facile sniping* (here) criticism based on ideological views but lacking careful thought
21 *kook* person who is crazy
25 *leaven sth.* ['levən] make sth. less heavy
26 *grim* miserable
29 *gadget* small and useful machine or tool

settled down to tenure and a Volvo (or maybe a Prius) in some leafy academic grove.

But as I said, the movie is not about him. He is, rather, the surprisingly engaging vehicle for some very disturbing information. His explanations of complex environmental phenomena – the jet stream has always been a particularly tough one for me to grasp – are clear, and while some of the visual aids are a little corny, most of the images are stark, illuminating and powerful.

I can't think of another movie in which the display of a graph elicited gasps of horror, but when the red lines showing the increasing rates of carbon-dioxide emissions and the corresponding rise in temperatures come on screen, the effect is jolting and chilling. Photographs of receding ice fields and glaciers – consequences of climate change that have already taken place – are as disturbing as speculative maps of submerged coastlines. The news of increased hurricane activity and warming oceans is all the more alarming for being delivered in Mr. Gore's matter-of-fact, scholarly tone.

He speaks of the need to reduce carbon-dioxide emissions as a "moral imperative," and most people who see this movie will do so out of a sense of duty, which seems to me entirely appropriate. Luckily, it happens to be a well-made documentary, edited crisply enough to keep it from feeling like 90 minutes of C-Span and shaped to give Mr. Gore's argument a real sense of drama. As unsettling as it can be, it is also intellectually exhilarating, and, like any good piece of pedagogy, whets the appetite for further study. This is not everything you need to know about global warming: that's the point. But it is a good place to start, and to continue, a process of education that could hardly be more urgent. "An Inconvenient Truth" is a necessary film.

From: The New York Times, *24 May 2006.*

32 *tenure* a teaching job
32 *Prius* ['praɪəs] type of car
32 *leafy academic grove* (here) pleasant small university
38 *corny* not original so it appears silly
43 *be jolting and chilling* come suddenly and cause a feeling of fear
53 *C-Span* a US TV Channel that only reports about politics
55 *whet the appetite increase* the desire for sth.

■ 1 *Multiple Choice*

Write down the letter of the correct answer.

A. *An Inconvenient Truth* is a film that should have never been made, because
   a. it is not based on sound science.
   b. it is not the job of filmmakers but of politicians to react to the new findings.
   c. the public is not interested in the topic.

B. However, we should be grateful that the film exists because
   a. politicians have not dealt with the problem of global warming.
   b. the retired politician, Al Gore, would not have anything else to do.
   c. scientists can inform the public about new findings in the field of global warming.

C. In the film, Al Gore
   a. is the central character. The film is basically about him and his life in and out of politics.
   b. appears as a stiff humourless speaker, as someone to make fun of rather than take seriously.
   c. presents his slide show on global warming, which he has already given many times over the last few years.

D. From his appearance in the film the viewer gets the impression that
   a. Al Gore would probably have been good as a university professor
   b. Al Gore is insecure. That is why he paces back and forth and fiddles with gadgets during his presentation.
   c. Al Gore should have remained in politics, because he has difficulties trying to keep the attention of his audience.

■ 2 Explain the seeming contradiction that – according to the author – *An Inconvenient Truth* is "a necessary film" (l. 62), although it "is a film that should never have been made" (ll. 2–3).

■ 3 Analyze the review and point out how the author tries to convince his readers of his opinion. In doing so mainly concentrate on the structure of the review.

■ 4 Implicitly the reader learns the arguments that opponents of the film bring forward. Write a review for someone who disproves of the film.

Al Gore's "Nine Inconvenient Untruths"

Al Gore's environmental documentary *An Inconvenient Truth* contains nine key scientific errors, a High Court judge ruled yesterday.

The judge declined to ban the Academy Award-winning film from British schools, but ruled that it can only be shown with guidance notes to prevent political indoctrination.

In the documentary, directed by Davis Guggenheim, the former US vice president and environmental activist calls on people to fight global warming because "humanity is sitting on a ticking time bomb".

But Judge Michael Burton ruled yesterday that errors had arisen "in the context of alarmism and exaggeration" in order to support Mr Gore's thesis on global warming.

His criticism followed an unsuccessful attempt by Stewart Dimmock, a Kent school governor, to block the Government's plan to screen the documentary in more than 3,500 secondary schools in England and Wales.

The father of two claimed *An Inconvenient Truth* included "serious scientific inaccuracies, political propaganda and sentimental mush".

The film's distributor, Paramount, warns in its synopsis of the film: "If the vast majority of the world's scientists are right, we have just ten years to avert a major catastrophe that could send our entire planet into a

17 *mush* thing that is too sentimental

tail-spin of epic destruction involving extreme weather, floods, droughts, epidemics and killer heat waves beyond anything we have ever experienced."

But the judge ruled that the "apocalyptic vision" presented in the film was politically partisan and thus not an impartial scientific analysis of climate change.

It is, he ruled, a "political film".

The nine alleged errors in the film

1. **Mr. Gore claims** that a sea-level rise of up to 20 feet would be caused by melting of either West Antarctica or Greenland "in the near future". **The judge said:** "This is distinctly alarmist and part of Mr. Gore's 'wake-up call'". He agreed that if Greenland melted it would release this amount of water – "but only after, and over, millennia". "The Armageddon scenario he predicts, insofar as it suggests that sea level rises of seven metres might occur in the immediate future, is not in line with the scientific consensus."
2. **The film claims** that low-lying inhabited Pacific atolls "are being inundated because of anthropogenic global warming" but **the judge ruled** there was no evidence of any evacuation having yet happened.
3. **The documentary speaks** of global warming "shutting down the Ocean Conveyor" – the process by which the Gulf Stream is carried over the North Atlantic to Western Europe. Citing the Intergovernmental Panel on Climate Change (IPCC), **the judge said** that it was "very unlikely" that the Ocean Conveyor, also known as the Meridional Overturning Circulation, would shut down in the future, though it might slow down.
4. **Mr. Gore claims** that two graphs, one plotting a rise in CO_2 and the other the rise in temperature over a period of 650,000 years, showed "an exact fit". **The judge said** that, although there was general scientific agreement that there was a connection, "the two graphs do not establish what Mr. Gore asserts".
5. **Mr. Gore says** the disappearance of snow on Mt Kilimanjaro was directly attributable to global warming, but **the judge ruled** that scientists have not established that the recession of snow on Mt Kilimanjaro is primarily attributable to human-induced climate change.
6. **The film contends** that the drying up of Lake Chad is a prime example of a catastrophic result of global warming but **the judge said** there was insufficient evidence, and that "it is apparently considered to be far more likely to result from other factors, such as population increase and over-grazing, and regional climate variability."
7. **Mr. Gore blames** Hurricane Katrina and the consequent devastation in New Orleans on global warming, but **the judge ruled** there was "insufficient evidence to show that".
8. **Mr. Gore cites** a scientific study that shows, for the first time, that polar bears were being found after drowning from "swimming long

21 *tail-spin* a bad situation that keeps getting worse
25 *partisan* strongly supporting a political party or ideology
38 *be inundated* be covered with a large amount of water
57 *contend* argue or state that sth. is true
61 *over-grazing* the destruction of grasslands by too many animals eating off the land

distances – up to 60 miles – to find the ice". **The judge said**: "The only scientific study that either side before me can find is one which indicates that four polar bears have recently been found drowned because of a storm." That was not to say there might not in future be drowning-related deaths of bears if the trend of regression of pack ice continued – "but it plainly does not support Mr. Gore's description".

9. **Mr. Gore said** that coral reefs all over the world were being bleached because of global warming and other factors. Again citing the IPCC, **the judge agreed** that, if temperatures were to rise by 1–3 degrees centigrade, there would be increased coral bleaching and mortality, unless the coral could adapt. However, he ruled that separating the impacts of stresses due to climate change from other stresses, such as over-fishing, and pollution was difficult.

From: Sally Peck, The Daily Telegraph, *11 October 2007.*

1 *Matching Exercise*

Match Dimmock's arguments for banning the film from English schools.

A. Gore's claim that the sea-level rise of 20 feet caused by melting of Greenland or Antartica will occur in the near future	a. However, it won't shut down but will only slow down.
B. Despite the considerable damage it caused, there is no evidence for the claim	b. but could also be due to population increase or natural climate variability.
C. The film claims that global warming might shut down the Ocean Conveyor.	c. is alarmist, because – although the fact itself is correct – it would happen only after thousands of years.
D. Despite the fact that scientists agree that there is a connection between the rise of CO_2 and the rise of temperature,	d. is wrong. The only study that exists indicates that some have drowned because of a storm.
E. The reason for the melting of glaciers and disappearance of snow on mountains	e. that Hurricane Katrina was a result of global warming.
F. The reason for the drying-up of Lake Chad might be global warming	f. might not primarily be due to human-caused climate change.
G. Despite the rise in sea levels, there is no indication	g. the graphs that Gore shows do not prove this assertion.
H. Gore's scientific study that there have been drowning-related deaths of polar bears because of the recession of the ice	h. is basically correct. However, the impacts of over-fishing and pollution must also be taken into account.
I. The claim that coral reefs are being bleached because of global warming	i. that low-lying areas in the Pacific are being flooded and therefore evacuated.

■ 2 Explain why the British judge ruled that the film can only be shown with guidance notes to prevent political indoctrination.

■ 3 Discuss the assertion that the film is "politically partisan" (l. 25) with reference to certain film scenes.

■ 4 Write a letter to the judge, in which you critically comment on his statements about the film. You can do research on the Internet to help you formulate your ideas.

Hot Chair Debate

Preparation

Group 1:

3 to 5 in the class prepare for the hot chair.
Prepare to defend Gore's position on climate change against critics. In doing so, all the members of the group should have read:

- An Inconvenient Truth about Al Gore (p. 43)
- Bush on Climate Change (p. 45)
- The Reception of the Film (p. 49)

Collect all the arguments that support Gore's view of climate change.

Then collect all the arguments that you find in these texts that might be used by opposing groups. Try to prepare counter-arguments. In doing so, refer to passages and diagrams from the film.

Group 2:

The rest of the class prepares for the group of critics. In doing so, all the members of the group should have read:

- An Inconvenient Truth about Al Gore (p. 43)
- Bush on Climate Change (p. 45)
- The Reception of the Film (p. 49)

Collect all the arguments that you find in these texts that might be used to criticize Gore's views on climate change. Then prepare critical questions for Gore.

The Hot Seat Debate:

- Put seats in a semi-circle around 3–5 chairs. These 3–5 chairs are taken by Gore and his "advisors". The other seats are taken by the critics.

- The critics are allowed to ask questions about Al Gore and his attitude towards and his contribution to climate change. Gore and his advisors have to defend themselves.

Writing a Resolution

■ 1 Have a look at the table from the pre-watching activities again (cf. p. 7). Add points that you have learned from the film and – if necessary – correct certain points.

■ 2 Write a resolution on global warming for a United Nations Conference. For help look at the information vocabulary boxes below.

INFO

What is a resolution?
A resolution is an official UN document submitted by one or more countries. It consists of one long sentence divided into clauses and sub-clauses. Each line is numbered and it is divided into two parts:

a. The Preambulatory Clauses
- describe the current situation and your attitude towards it
- begin with a present or past participle (Approving/Alarmed by)
- are separated by commas

b. The Operative Clauses
- say which kind of action you want to take (each clause must contain only one action)
- begin with a verb in the 3rd person singular (Suggests/Hopes)
- are separated by semicolon
- are numbered
- Important: A resolution must not reproach or condemn, but promote peaceful solutions to world problems.

Useful phrases for the preambulatory clauses			
Acknowledging	Deeply disturbed by	Having considered	Observing
Alarmed by	(Deeply) regretting	Having examined	Pointing out
Approving of	Deploring	Having heard	Reaffirming
Aware of	Desiring	Having received	Realizing
Believing	Expecting	Having studied	Recalling
Bearing in mind	Expressing its appreciation	Keeping in mind	Recognizing
Confident	Expressing its satisfaction	Noting further	Referring
Contemplating	Fulfilling	Noting with appreciation	Reminding
Declaring	Fully aware	Noting with approval	Seeking
(Deeply) concerned	Further recalling	Noting with deep concern	Taking into account
Deeply conscious of	Guided by	Noting with regret	Taking into consideration
(Deeply) convinced	Having adopted	Noting with satisfaction	Welcoming

Useful verbs for the operative phrases			
Accepts	Deplores	(Further) recommends	(Strongly) urges
Approves of	Designates	(Further) requests	Suggests
Asks	Encourages	(Further) resolves	Supports
Authorizes	Endorses	Hopes	Trusts
Calls for/upon	Expresses its appreciation	Proposes	Transmits
Congratulates	Expresses its hope	Regrets	
Confirms	(Further) invites	(Strongly) affirms	
Declares accordingly	(Further) proclaims	(Strongly) condemns	

Start your resolution like this:

FORUM: Environment Commission

QUESTION OF: Global Warming

SUBMITTED BY: Germany (or any other country or countries)

THE ENVIRONMENT COMMISSION

1. Alarmed by the melting of Larson Ice Shelf in Antarctica, [...]
2. Deeply concerned about the effect the melting of land-based ice has on the sea-level, [...]

    1. Appeals to the US government to sign the Kyoto protocol;
    2. Suggests that all governments consider imposing taxes on

        a. high mileage cars
        b. companies that do not meet the standards for reducing CO_2

■ **3** Prepare a speech on your resolution, in which you try to convince your listeners to approve of and sign it. In doing so refer to certain clauses and explain why they are important.

Melissa Etheridge: I Need to Wake Up

Have I been sleeping?
I've been so still
Afraid of crumbling
Have I been careless?
Dismissing all the distant rumblings
Take me where I am supposed to be
To comprehend the things that I can't see
Cause I need to move
I need to wake up
I need to change
I need to shake up
I need to speak out
Something's got to break up
I've been asleep
And I need to wake up
Now
And as a child
I danced like it was 1999
My dreams were wild
The promise of this new world
Would be mine
Now I am throwing off the carelessness of youth
To listen to an inconvenient truth
That I need to move
I need to wake up
I need to change
I need to shake up
I need to speak out
Something's got to break up
I've been asleep
And I need to wake up
Now
I am not an island
I am not alone
I am my intentions
Trapped here in this flesh and bone
And I need to move
I need to wake up
I need to change
I need to shake up
I need to speak out
Something's got to break up
I've been asleep
And I need to wake up
Now
I want to change
I need to shake up
I need to speak out
Oh, Something's got to break up
I've been asleep
And I need to wake up
Now

5 *dismiss sth.* refuse to consider sth.
5 *rumbling (n)* noise that shows that a difficult situation is developing

■ **1** Summarize what the song is about.
■ **2** Analyze the lyrics. Explain how the message of the song is emphasized by the form and the rhetorical devices.
■ **3** Listen to the music on the video. Analyze the mood that is created by the music. Do you think that it underlines the message of the song?
■ **4** Describe the possible setting for the video and make a story board for a possible video. If you like, you can even film your own video. Make sure that the message of the song is underlined.
■ **5** Compare your ideas to the video on the DVD.

Recent Ecological Disasters

Africa ...

Head north from Nairobi toward Mount Kenya and almost invariably you'll hit weather. Fog, rain, hail, even snow, all unusual for the equator but a blessing for Mount Kenya's farmers, who export coffee, roses, green beans and peas to Europe. Once you pass the mountain and descend onto the dusty Samburu plain, however, the weather evaporates. The first town you reach is Archer's Post, a collection of dusty shacks around a truck stop. From there, says elder Leadisimo Lehgalee, 69, the Samburu are forced to watch the daily deluge over Mount Kenya while enduring a drought on their land that began in 1997. Inevitably, jealousy and desperation turn to enmity. "We rob them," says Lehgalee. "And they rob us back. We raid each other's cattle, and we fight, we kill, and we die. That's the Samburu life."

The urge to appropriate what's on the other side of the fence rules much of the Sahel, the belt of scrub and semidesert that runs across Africa between the Sahara to the north and the plains to the south. The wars in Darfur and Somalia and between northern and southern Sudan all have roots in tribal competition for land and livestock. In northern Kenya, scores die every year in clashes over watering holes and cattle. And if all that weren't enough, lately the Sahara and the Sahel have attracted a new fearsome breed of outsiders, such as al-Qaeda and South America's cocaine cartels, who use the lawless wastes as sanctuaries and smuggling routes.

Africa's deserts, in short, are all kinds of dangerous. And climate change means the badlands are growing. The U.N. Food and Agriculture Organization says that on the southern edge of the Sahara, an area the size of Somalia has become desert in the past 50 years. The U.N. Environment Programme (UNEP) says 14 African countries currently experience water scarcity or stress, a number that will rise to 25 by 2025. In a May 2008 report, the U.N. Convention to Combat Desertification (UNCCD) said 46 % of Africa is threatened by land degradation. UNCCD executive secretary Luc Gnacadja concluded that desertification is "the greatest environmental challenge of our times."

The coming climate crisis will have a massive human cost. The Intergovernmental Panel on Climate Change (IPCC) says that by 2020, "agricultural production, including access to food, in many African countries is projected to be severely compromised." The effects of climate change, including rising sea levels and flooding as well as droughts and

1 *head* go
3 *fog* Nebel
3 *hail* Hagel
12 *elder* leader of a tribe
14 *deluge* large amount of water
18 *urge* strong desire
18 *appropriate sth.* take sth. and make it yours
23 *scores* many
26 *wastes* area where few people live
35 *degradation* process of becoming worse or damaged

desertification, would put at risk of hunger 80 million to 120 million people, of whom 70 % to 80 % would be Africans, according to the IPCC. Food prices are likely to rise, and with them poverty and disease: mosquitoes and locusts thrive as temperatures go up.

As Samburu's neighbors know, tough places produce desperate, angry people. Unlivable places produce refugees. In a May 2005 study, Oxford and Duke University environmentalist Norman Myers calculated that there were 16 million "environmental refugees" in Africa in 1995 and predicted that number would double by this year. In April 2007, 11 former U.S. admirals and generals described a warming world as a "threat incubator" in a report for the think tank CNA Corp. The same month, the U.N. Security Council held a debate on how climate change can start wars.

46 *thrive* live well
53 *think tank* Expertenkommission

From: Alex Perry, "Land of Hope", Time Magazine, *12 December 2010.*

Pakistan ...

Pakistan floods

Flood levels in Pakistan are expected to surge even higher along parts of the already dangerously swollen Indus river. The National Disaster Management Authority (NDMA) said "major peaks" were expected on Friday and next week in Punjab and Sindh provinces.

The region's worst flooding in 80 years has affected 14 million people and killed 1,600, according to the UN. Doctors say that malaria, diarrhoea and gastroenteritis are growing threats. [...]

NDMA spokesman Ahmed Kamal said: "There can be further devastation as we are expecting two major peaks in the Indus system. He said places downstream of the Kotri barrage – a flood barrier in Sindh – and areas on either side of the Taunsa barrage in Punjab were likely to take the brunt of this surge. [...]

The UN on Wednesday launched a $459m (£294m) appeal for emergency aid but says billions will be needed in the long-term.

Meanwhile, medics in a relief camp in southern Punjab told the BBC the main challenges they face are gastroenteritis, diarrhoea and skin infections. But they are also increasingly worried about malaria, which is being worsened by all the stagnant water.

2 *surge* get larger quickly
11 *diarrhoea* [ˌdaɪə'rɪə] Durchfall
14 *peak* high point
17 *take the brunt of sth.* receive the main force of sth. unpleasant
23 *stagnant* (of water) that does not move

As a US ship with more helicopters and 1,000 Marines arrived to boost the relief efforts, Pakistan's political leaders pledged that all aid distribution would be transparent.

Prime Minister Gilani said: "Whatever you give, we will give an account of every single penny."

From: "Pakistan Floods: Two 'Major Peaks" due on Indus River", website of the BBC, 13 August 2010. © BBC 2011

The United States ...

Bad Times on the Gulf

In 2010 a leak from an oil well caused extensive damage to the Gulf of Mexico.

There's a world of difference between the impact of an oil spill and a deadly hurricane. And the White House hopes it stays that way.

As President Obama, who will visit the Gulf region on Sunday morning, has stepped up his administration's response to the oil leak in the Gulf of Mexico, ordering a moratorium on new offshore drilling leases and dispatching cabinet secretaries and cargo planes to the region, the White House is also trying to avert the kind of political damage inflicted on former President George W. Bush by his administration's slow response to Hurricane Katrina. [...]

Mr. Obama, for his part, vowed, for the second time in two days that his administration would respond aggressively to the oil spill. He maintained that he continued to "believe that domestic oil production is an important part of our overall strategy for energy security," addressing concerns about whether the administration would stick with its plan to increase drilling in the gulf.

But administration officials left open the possibility that they might reconsider the decision to expand offshore drilling if conditions in the gulf worsened. Mr. Gibbs said there would be "an extensive environmental review before deciding" on issuing new drilling leases. [...]

Natural disasters provide great opportunities, or great peril, for presidents. President Bush's slow response to Hurricane Katrina in 2005, magnified by his now-infamous "You're doing a heck of a job, Brownie" praise of his FEMA director, Michael Brown, cemented an impression that his administration failed to act with enough urgency to address the suffering of tens of thousands of people.

The widening environmental calamity in the gulf is the first time Mr. Obama has confronted a domestic disaster. Complicating the White House response is the fact that the spill occurred just a month after the president announced he was expanding offshore drilling.

5 *moratorium* befristete Einstellung
5 *drill* bohren
6 *lease* contract to do sth. for a period of time
6 *dispatch sb.* send sb.
22 *a heck of* (infml) a very good

Officials note that a key difference between the spill and Hurricane Katrina is the pace of the onslaught of the disaster. While the hurricane hit the Gulf Coast in a fury, the oil has – literally – crept to the shores of the gulf. While the eventual harm from the leak could outstrip that of the Exxon Valdez accident in Alaska, that will not be known for weeks, if not months.

While characterizing the Obama administration's response to the spill as intense, Bill Eichbaum of the World Wildlife Fund said the disaster showed that the expansion plans were a bad idea.

"This spill in the gulf is like having a heart attack in New York City," he said. "Everything is there that you need to fix it. If you have a spill in the Arctic, it's like having a heart attack on the North Pole. There's nothing there to help you fix it."

From: Helene Cooper, "Shadow of Hurricane Katrina Hangs Over Obama After Spill", New York Times, *30 April 2010.*

Text: Africa

■ 1 Explain the consequences that the droughts in Africa have for the population.

■ 2 Summarize the predictions that the UNEP has made for the future of Africa.

■ 3 Explain the idea that a warming world is a "threat incubator" (l. 53).

Text: Pakistan

■ 1 Summarize the consequences that the flood in Pakistan had on the people there.

Text: The USA

■ 1 Explain the meaning of the original title of the article (cf. the source at the end of the text).

■ 2 What is Obama's attitude towards offshore oil drilling?

■ 3 According to the text, what seem to be the most important concerns of American governments when faced with an ecological catastrophe?

Mediation

Imagine a friend in the USA sends you an email after watching *An Inconvenient Truth* in class. In this email he writes the following:

"We watched Al Gore's movie 'An Inconvenient Truth' in class and we are really concerned about climate change and its consequences. However, many Americans still question the seriousness of the problem and have no intention of changing their lifestyles. That's why we, as a class, want to start a school project on climate change to make the citizens of our town aware of the problem. I am writing to you to see if you have any ideas that could help us."

You find a website with the following information about a school project on climate change. Read the text and inform your friend about the school project. Tell him how and where it was organized, and what information it offered.

„Klimawandel – wir werden aktiv"

Jeden Tag Fleisch, ist das nötig? So steht's auf dem blauen Plakat unter „Tipps für ein klimabewusstes Essen", umrandet von bunten Früchten und Gemüsegirlanden. Gleich daneben „Die weitreichenden Folgen übermäßigen Fleischkonsums bei der Massentierhaltung".

Klimaretter unterwegs

Schülerinnen und Schüler des Soziologie-Leistungskurses im Gymnasium Obervieland – alle im weißen T-Shirt mit der Aufschrift „Klimaretter" – haben im Rahmen ihres Projekttages „Klimaretter 2010" eine bemerkenswerte Ausstellung im Cinemaxx Bremen präsentiert. Kleine Themen-Inseln im Oberen Foyer des Cinemaxx belegen eindringlich: Unsere Erde ist in Gefahr, wenn nicht endlich etwas geschieht. Und zwar in den Industrieländern, denn sie sind Verursacher des Klimawandels, der für die Länder der südlichen Halbkugel noch viel verheerendere Folgen hat.

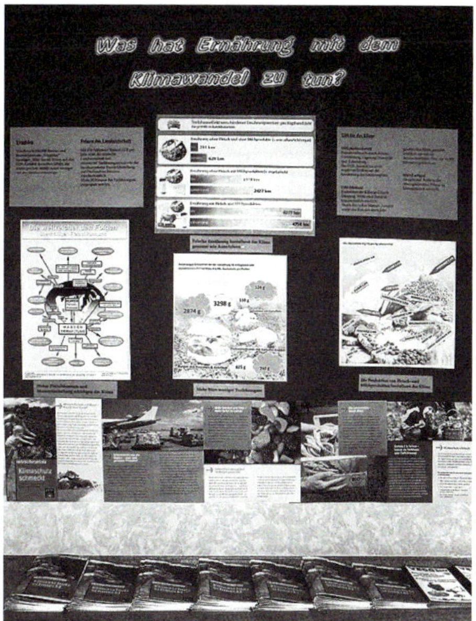

Kritischer Blick in die Zukunft

Den Ausschlag gab Al Gores Film „Eine unbequeme Wahrheit". „Danach", sagt Lehrer Dieter Mazur, „waren viele Schülerinnen und Schüler wirklich geschockt und wollten etwas tun." Dann kam noch die gescheiterte Klimakonferenz in Kopenhagen dazu, „und die Idee des Projekttages war geboren". Sie recherchierten über globale Erwärmung, Mobilität, Wasserressourcen, erneuerbare Energien und ethische Fragen zum Klimawandel, über Visionen von unserer Mobilität im Jahr 2040, Ernährung und ökologischen Fußabdruck.

Dieses Thema gerät zunehmend mehr in den Blickpunkt. „Falsche Ernährung belastet das Klima genauso wie Autofahren", weiß Maria inzwischen und ein ‚Hamburger' ist deutlich klimafeindlicher als eine Gemüsepfanne. „Aber es ist schwer, diesen Zusammenhang bewusst zu machen", sagt Katharina, die von der Dringlichkeit des Themas überzeugt ist: „Etwas tun gegen den Klimawandel, ja. Aber dafür auf den Burger zu verzichten? Nee, das wollen sie nicht."

Verantwortung

Jeder einzelne kann etwas tun – aus unterschiedlichen ethischen und religiösen Blickwinkeln. Das zeigt die Themeninsel Verantwortung: „Künftige Generationen müssen vor der Gefahr einer tristen Existenz in einer immer heißer werdenden Welt bewahrt werden ..." ist da zu lesen, und weil man am besten bei sich selber anfangen soll, haben die Schülerinnen und Schüler ihr Umweltverhalten in einer Fragebogenaktion unter die Lupe genommen. Ergebnis: „Grenzwertig, aber wir hoffen, mit diesem Fragebogen die Schüler dazu bewegen zu können, noch umweltbewusster zu handeln".

Unbequeme Wahrheit

Unterschiedliche Exponate – eine ganze Batterie von Mineralwasserflaschen oder eine Pyramide mit 30 Tipps zum Energiesparen – Texte, Fotos und Plakate veranschaulichen die „Unbequeme Wahrheit", die darüber hinaus im gleichnamigen Film von Al Gore, dem ehemaligen Vizepräsidenten der USA, mit Statistiken und wissenschaftlichen Fakten belegt wird. Ein Film, der „sprachlos gemacht hat, weil er das Klimaproblem in seiner ganzen Dramatik beleuchtet", sagt ein Schüler.

Politische Gäste

Diese Dramatik konnten Schülerinnen und Schüler anschließend mit Umweltsenator Reinhard Loske und BUND-Geschäftsführer Martin Rode diskutieren, um zum Abschluss auf dem Schulgelände zum Schutz des bedrohten Klimas Bäume zu pflanzen: Dort wachsen jetzt drei Erlen, betreut von Schülern der Integrierten Stadtteilschule, die zum Start zwölf Wassereimer überreicht bekamen. Und im Sommer geht's im Rahmen des Leistungskurses nach Bremerhaven, ins Klimahaus.

From: a project by the Gymnasium Obervieland, the website of Veggiday, 2009"Klimawandel – wir werden aktiv"